asian cook

Terry Tan

photography by Michael Paul

asian cook

jacqui
small

First published in 2003 by Jacqui Small,
an imprint of Aurum Press Ltd, 25 Bedford Avenue,
London WC1B 3AT.

Publisher Jacqui Small
Art Director Valerie Fong
Tools Photography Nat Rea
Food Styling Terry Tan, Kit Chan and Emi Kazuko
Project Editor Jenni Muir
Copy Editor Marion Moisy
Production Geoff Barlow

British Library Cataloguing-in-Publication Data
A catalogue record for this book is available from the British Library.

ISBN 1 903221 12 9

Printed and bound in China

RECIPE NOTES Oils Unless otherwise specified, all recipes require the use of
a light oil with a neutral taste, such as corn, sunflower, grapeseed, safflower or
groundnut oil. Use olive oil only where
specified. **Eggs** are large. **Sugar** is
granulated white or caster
sugar unless otherwise specified. **Pepper** is freshly ground
black pepper unless otherwise
specified. **Spoon measurements**
Recipes use standard measuring
spoons; note that table cutlery varies
in capacity. Spoon measurements
are level. **Preparation time** includes
cooking time; soaking or marinating
time is given separately.

contents

6 Introduction

9 China

45 Japan and Korea

77 India, Pakistan and Sri Lanka

99 Indochina
including Thailand, Vietnam, Laos,
Myanmar and Kampuchea

119 Southeast Asia
including Singapore, Malaysia
and Indonesia

141 Suppliers

142 Acknowledgements and bibliography

143 Index

introduction

Most people in the West believe that Asian kitchens are exotic, full of strange and rustic implements, of granite mortars that need forklifts to move them and cast-iron woks that rust before you can say 'stir-fry'. True, some tools used in Asian cooking can seem esoteric, even mystifying, but most are very simple to use. Take the granite mortar and pestle: it has been around for centuries and is small and light enough for even a child to use. I inherited mine from my grandmother, which makes it older than I am! It has now worn to a silky smoothness and grinds spices and aromatics beautifully into emulsion-like pastes.

It is fascinating and therapeutic to grind, grate, slice, and chop using age-old tools and implements. They seem to impart an extra and mysterious dimension of flavour to the dish cooked, and, despite the introduction of food processors, true quality and authenticity for many dishes are often only achievable by using the traditional tools that have stood the test of time. Most are easy to use, and few require painstaking instructions; however, frequent practice helps produce perfect results. In the pantheon of good, authentic cooking, there is much to be said for using implements designed for specific tasks. Even better, they make wonderful heirlooms to hand down to the next generation.

For generations, Asians have used a wide range of the tools chronicled in this book. Some implements have been threatened with extinction, but more than a few have been saved from the back burner of history, modernised, and even adapted into exciting new electrical appliances. Much of what can be found in Asian kitchens is available in specialty stores and ethnic supermarkets, many of which now have their own web sites. Some tools may be harder to track down, but most avid cooks agree this is all part of the fun of exploring the cuisines of other lands.

Geographically, the Asia we refer to here embraces China; India, Pakistan, and Sri Lanka; Japan and Korea; the five distinct countries of Myanmar (formerly Burma), Laos, Kampuchea (formerly Cambodia), Thailand, and Vietnam; and the islands of the Indonesian archipelago and neighbouring Malaysia and Singapore, collectively known as Southeast Asia. Although Laotian and Kampuchean cooking are relatively unknown in the Western world, they share common characteristics with their neighbouring countries.

Even though contemporary lifestyles dictate the need for high-tech appliances, Asian kitchens still contain tools evocative of the agrarian way of life. There is a special relationship between their aesthetic and their functionality. For instance, banana leaf serves as a mat for steamed coconut rice while imparting a distinctive fragrance to the dish. When Thai sticky rice is served in a woven banana-leaf basket, the flavour is subtly enhanced.

High-tech appliances may well make short work of food processing, but speed is not the be-all and end-all of kitchen craft. The true enjoyment of food often dictates that some effort must be made. The split-second timing of stir-frying, the consistency and delicacy of dumpling dough, and the smoothness of spice pastes are all dependent on using the correct tool. Even the simplest items can be used ingeniously. Two-foot-long chopsticks are a good example. When you deep-fry food, if you pick up the cooked morsels using a conventional ladle or tongs, you run the risk of hot fat splattering on you. With very long chopsticks, the distance between cook and wok ensures that there is no danger.

Several of the tools and foods featured in this book have traditional symbolic, religious, or mystical significance, and it can only enhance your enjoyment to dwell a little on the hidden symbolism. Every Japanese dish reflects a mood dictated by a season, whereas the Chinese people love roundness because it symbolizes eternity. Whatever your reason for exploring the East, be it buying a wok, re-creating food sampled on vacation, or looking for an exciting wrap for dumplings, I hope you enjoy using this book and the tools featured in it.

material choice

This list explains the pros and cons of the principal materials from which the eclectic range of Asian cooking equipment is made or naturally derived, and gives guidance on care, preparation, cleaning and storing.

aluminium

Uses Pots, steamers, tiffin carriers, storage tins, cake moulds, ladles and woks.

Pros Cheap, lightweight, conducts heat well and evenly as long as the gauge is heavy enough.

Cons Reacts with acidic elements in food juices and therefore will discolour certain foods or impart a metallic taste. The metal tends to discolour and pit. Thin-gauge aluminium warps easily and heats unevenly.

Care Wash with hot soapy water, using a scouring pad if necessary. Remove stains by boiling in a weak solution of vinegar or cream of tartar.

anodised aluminium

Uses As for aluminium.

Pros This electro-chemical process gives aluminium a hard, dense oxide coating that resists corrosion. Hard anodising produces a coating and changes the molecular structure of the aluminium, making it harder than steel while maintaining excellent heat distribution.

Cons Dishwasher detergents cause coloured anodised aluminium pans to fade.

Care Wash anodised aluminium with hot soapy water. Do not use scouring pads.

bamboo

Uses Utensils, steamers and lids, barbecue skewers.

Pros Cheap, portable and non-reactive to foods, its porous nature is an advantage when used for steaming.

Cons Can get brittle with frequent use, relatively short life, will warp and burn if not handled carefully.

Care Wash with hot water only as the material is porous and absorbs cleaning fluids.

brass

Uses Cake moulds, pestles and mortars, karahis.

Pros An alloy of copper and zinc, with other metals such as aluminium and tin added for strength and anti-corrosion properties. It is tough, corrosion- and rust-free, beautiful and functional.

Cons Can be extremely heavy.

Care Wash with hot soapy water and detergent.

cast iron

Uses Pots, pans, griddles, grill pans, casseroles, teppanyaki hot plates, teapots

Pros Durable, strong, does not warp, conducts heat evenly and retains it well. Marvellous for long, slow cooking using minimal fat.

Cons Very heavy, so best for a pan that remains fairly static during cooking, such as casseroles. Its density makes it slow to heat. If dropped on a hard floor, it may break. If uncoated (for example, if it does not have an enamel or non-stick surface) it must be seasoned with oil to prevent sticking and rusting.

Care Avoid uncoated cast iron. Wipe with paper towels. Remove stuck-on food by lightly scouring under hot running water. Dry well and coat with oil before storing, Brush the cooking surface with oil before each use, then wipe off before adding oil for cooking. Wash coated cast iron with hot, soapy water but do not scour. To remove stubborn residue, leave the pan for an hour or so to soak.

clay and terracotta

Uses Cooking pots, yogurt pots, mortars, dishes.

Pros Attractive, rustic, non-reactive. Chinese clay pots have supportive wire mesh to help prevent breakage.

Cons Cracks easily if roughly handled. Clay pots do not take well to direct flame cooking and are best used over charcoal embers or in the oven.

Care Wash and dry but never use detergents as the material is absorbent. Dishwasher safe. Never store stacked one in another as this will cause cracking.

coconut shell

Uses The outer hard casing of the coconut is shaped into all sorts of implements including bowls, ladles, serving utensils, spoons and spatulas.

Pros Non-reactive, inexpensive, rustic, versatile.

Cons Can be hard to come by, cracks easily, few matching sets. Some discolouration can occur when coconut shell is used for spices.

Care Wash with hot soapy water, and to remove stuck-on food, scrub or scour but not with detergents as the material is absorbent.

copper

Uses Karahis, moulds, wire mesh ladles.

Pros The traditional choice of Western chefs but used much less in Asia because of high cost. Some utensils have a light copper plating but it is mainly used for mesh. Never rusts or turns brittle.

Cons Pricey and needs cosseting.

Care Wash with hot, soapy water. Never use scouring pads. Soak with a little vinegar and dry with a soft cloth to bring up the shine.

earthenware

Uses Casseroles, herbal pots, pestles and mortars.

Pros Non-reactive, cheap, porous, retains heat and moisture well. Excellent for slow, moist cooking in the oven, for use in a microwave and on the stovetop for gently simmered soups and stews if protected.

Cons Dislikes sudden or extreme temperature changes. It is not flameproof, but good quality earthenware can be used on a heat diffuser over a low flame.

Care Wash glazed, or partially glazed, pots with hot, soapy water without scouring. Completely unglazed pots should be scrubbed clean with salt water. Do not use detergent as this taints the food.

granite and stoneware

Uses An ancient material used mainly in heavy grinding tools, and as serving dishes such as the Korean bibimbap bowl.

Pros Virtually indestructible, but will break if dropped from a height. Does not stain, and is non-toxic and non-reactive.

Cons Heavy, clumsy and difficult to clean.

Care Wash with hot water and a light detergent. Scrub out with a Brillo pad after grinding spices and soak in hot water for an hour to remove strong smells.

lacquer ware

Uses Plates, bowls, bento boxes, trays and other serving dishes. The sap from the lacquer tree is applied in many layers, then heated and allowed to dry.

Pros Beautiful, lightweight, portable, delicate but tough enough for dishwashers. Retains heat well, does not stain, non-toxic and non-reactive.

Cons Cannot be used for cooking, may chip if knocked or dropped.

Care Wash with hot soapy water and dry with a soft cloth to prevent staining.

leaves, dried

Uses Mainly from bamboo and lotus plants, dried leaves are used for wrapping savoury and sweet dishes that are then steamed or boiled.

Pros Impart distinctive fragrance, have a long shelf life if stored properly. Cheap and disposable.

Cons Crack and tear easily if not handled gently.

Care Must be kept in a cool, dry place.

leaves, dried basketware

Uses Many types of dried leaves are employed in the endless range of baskets used throughout Asia. Dried leaves of the pandanus family, usually found in mangrove swamps, coconut tree, rattan plant, bamboo and other broad types are woven into baskets of varying shapes and sizes, fans and food containers.

Pros They are relatively cheap (except when crafted and sold as exotic ornaments in gift shops). Excellent for steaming dryish dishes and serving. Unless waxed or otherwise treated with a coating, they do not react to cooking agents such as oil and vinegar, except for taking on a dark tan after use.

Cons They are not everlasting, being of a handicraft nature, and strips may come away after a while. They can become misshapen too.

Care Easy to wash and dry but not dishwasher safe because of the delicate weave.

leaves, fresh

Uses Leaves such as banana, pandanus (screwpine), bamboo and yam are used for wrapping, encasing, and perfuming foods, especially when steaming. Banana leaves are also cut into large pieces and employed as serving plates in tropical parts of Asia.

Pros Although scented, some fresh leaves are not edible, due to their fibrous nature. They are inexpensive and

disposable, and give a natural, authentic presentation.

Cons Fresh leaves are delicate, tear easily, and have a short shelf life. Some are only available fresh in the country in which they are grown.

Care Keep wrapped in a cool dry place for 3-4 days.

porcelain

Uses Plates, bowls, spoons, rice scoops and tureens.

Pros Can be delicate or tough depending on manufacture. Chinese and Japanese porcelain have been famous for centuries for their beauty and function. Very aesthetic, elegant, retains heat well but cool to the touch. Non-porous and non-reactive. Microwave friendly, except those with metallic paints.

Cons Should not be used over direct heat, fragile, and needs careful cleaning.

Care Wash in hot soapy water, soak to remove stuck-on food, dishwasher safe unless otherwise specified.

stainless steel

Uses Pots, pans, woks, ladles, scoops, serving dishes, storage containers, knives and cleavers.

Pros One of the toughest and most enduring materials, used in a wide range of tools and utensils. Contains chrome, which is what makes it stainless. Pristine-looking, long lasting and hygienic, rustproof and non-reactive. Immune to corrosion and pitting. Stainless steel utensils also contain nickel, described as 18/10, which means the ratio of chrome to nickel is 18 per cent and 10 per cent respectively. The stainless steel used in knives contains a lower level of chrome (at least 12 per cent) and 0.15-0.8 per cent carbon which gives it strength, as in professional Japanese carbon-steel knives. Because of the reduction in chrome, such items are more prone to staining.

Cons Stainless steel is a poor and uneven conductor of heat, but some woks and pots are made with a sandwich base of aluminium or copper to alleviate this problem. Good stainless steel utensils have a base containing at least 5 mm of aluminium or 3 mm of copper. Stainless steel is not entirely stainless and will discolour if left in contact with hard water, salt water, acidic juices or even some detergents if not rinsed out thoroughly after washing. Small pits may form.

Care Clean with hot soapy water, using a nylon scourer if necessary. Avoid bleach and harsh abrasives. Soak stuck-on foods and remove stubborn stains with a proprietary stainless steel cleaner.

wood

Uses Asian woods come in a range of types and varying degrees of hardness. They are used in cake moulds, trays, bowls, pot covers, steamer trivets, chopsticks, pot rests, tongs and rolling pins.

Pros Durable, inexpensive, non-reactive.

Cons Can be heavy, prone to discolouration if used with highly coloured ingredients.

Care Wash with hot soapy water, and scrub gently with a soft brush, especially when cleaning cake moulds with deeply etched, intricate designs.

china

china and its regions

'If there be only one note, there can be no music. If there be one flavour, there would be no satisfaction. If sugar is added to vinegar there would be the universal harmony of sweet and sour.' So said Yen Tzu, a disciple of Confucius, circa 600BC. This is the philosophy that underscores Chinese cuisine.

China is a vast country with enormous climatic and geographical variations. The cuisine has evolved over more than 3000 years and developed in an environment of constant flux with occasional periods of relative permanence. Today, ancient traditions and culinary innovations exist in delicious synergy.

Some 80 per cent of the 1.6 billion people still live a rural life engaged in agriculture. Despite a shortage of fertile arable land, Chinese farmers have learnt to nourish their terrain to produce bountiful harvests. Centuries-old terraced paddy fields maximise the use of water, even though there are frequent droughts. Despite the advent of refrigeration, Chinese people still insist on the freshest foods available and often shop several times a day to ensure this.

There are distinct regional schools in Chinese cuisine that run in line with the geographical boundaries of the Northern, Eastern, Southern and Western regions, better known as Beijing, Shanghainese, Cantonese and Sichuan cuisine respectively. Each is steeped in indigenous traditions. There are also lesser-known types such as the Muslim school of Northeast China, Hunanese, Hainanese (of Hainan Island) and several sub-schools within the southern Chinese province of Guangdong. Hong Kong, though a part of South China, has also evolved its own distinctive style.

The name of China's northern capital city has undergone no less than eight changes since it was first named Chi in 481BC. At various stages throughout the next 2500 years of political upheaval and other changes, it has been called Yenking, Chungtu, Tatu and Khanbalyk (both under the rule of Kublai Khan), Peking, Peiping and finally now Beijing.

Severe winters, short growing seasons and an arid climate have created a hearty cuisine. The staples grown throughout the region are wheat, millet and soy beans. Rice does not grow happily here and therefore rarely features in northern Chinese meals; the preference is for steamed wheat flour buns and noodles.

Northern cuisine is regarded as the most sophisticated of all, although it is robust and features simple ingredients. Its chief characteristic is the frequent and lavish use of soy bean paste, which is the basis of many well-known sauces including Hoi Sin and Yellow Bean. More influenced by the vast hinterland of Mongolia and beyond than the sea on its eastern shores, Northern Chinese menus are rich in lamb and duck, as well as roasted, braised and barbecued dishes. The world-famous Peking Duck is regarded as a national treasure.

The Yangtse River, China's longest waterway, leaves its mountain source in the Tibetan Plateau and flows through Sichuan before ending in the East China Sea just north of Shanghai. There is a vast

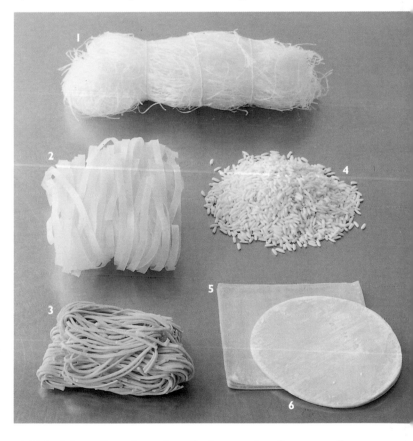

ABOVE: 1 bean thread noodles, 2 rice noodles, 3 egg noodles, 4 rice, 5 egg dumpling wrappers, 6 rice dumpling wrappers.
OPPOSITE: 1 baby bok choy, 2 mustard greens, 3 mangetout, 4 spring onions, 5 beansprouts.

network of lakes and tributaries in Eastern China, which is a leading agricultural region boasting some of the most fertile land in the country. Barley, wheat, rice, corn, sweet potatoes, peanuts and soy beans grow there in abundance. The region offers diverse cooking styles but all emphasise freshness and pure, natural flavours. Eastern China's stir-fried dishes are often plain, seasoned only with soy sauce and pepper. Lotus plants grow profusely in the ponds, lakes and streams, so many dishes are wrapped in lotus leaves and steamed.

The mountains of the warmer southern reaches of Eastern China feature many tea plantations. Fujian is perhaps the best-known of China's tea-growing provinces. Trade of the precious leaf with Europe in the early 19th century brought prosperity to the local residents, whose leisured classes were subsequently able to cultivate a fine taste for exquisite

ABOVE: **1** dark soy sauce, **2** oyster sauce, **3** bamboo shoots, **4** salted and fermented black beans, **5** light soy sauce, **6** hoisin sauce, **7** sesame oil, **8** five-spice powder, **9** Sichuan pepper, **10** water chestnuts, **11** white sesame seeds, **12** fresh ginger root, **13** dried Chinese mushrooms.

cooking. Fujian chefs are extremely fond of pork, using all the offal in highly imaginative ways, including dishes of steamed pig's blood. The long coastline, riverine areas and freshwater lakes are fecund with the seafood that also typifies this cuisine.

In the West, Sichuan has a tongue-tingling reputation as a fiery cauldron of chilli peppers. However chillies are not the be-all and end-all of the region's cooking, and several festive and banquet dishes are completely devoid of fire. The purpose of chilli peppers is not, as can sometimes seem the case, to paralyse the tongue but to stimulate the palate, making it more sensitive and receptive to the multiple flavours. Many of the sauces are a hotpotch of

hot, sweet, sour, aromatic and fragrant flavours, and Sichuanese dishes often break traditional culinary rules to brilliant effect. The range of dishes is delectable, from exquisite Jade Shrimps and Fire-exploded Kidney Flowers to popular Sweet and Sour Pork, Aromatic Crispy Duck, and Hot and Sour Soup. A spread of cold dishes is typically served at the start of a Sichuanese feast to tempt the palate.

The name Sichuan literally means 'Four Rivers', though there are more than twice this number, all tributaries of the mighty Yangtse River. A region of searingly hot summers and mild winters, it supports an astonishing range of plant foods and a wealth of subtropical fruits including oranges, limes, apples, plums and lychees. Sichuan teas are also justly famous, especially those from the West Lake area. The supreme variety is Dragon Well tea.

Historically, the southern province of Guangdong was allied to the former Guangxi province, now an autonomous region. Lying in the shadow of the Guangdong-Guangxi Mountains, the region is crisscrossed by three tributaries of the Yangtse, the best-known being the Pearl River that has given its name to soy sauce and other products.

Rice is the dominant grain. Peanuts, coconuts, pineapple, sugar cane, tea and coffee, as well as tobacco and rubber plants, are grown in abundance. There was much contact with Indian, Persian and Arab traders before the 15th century and, latterly, Portuguese, British, Dutch and French entrepreneurs called regularly.

The magic of this region's cooking, usually termed Cantonese, is concentrated on texture. Natural flavours are not altered and preparation is kept to a minimum. Absolute freshness is vital. The aim is to control crispness and subtlety, but perhaps the most distinctive aspect of Cantonese cuisine is savouriness. Seafood flavours are often incorporated into meat cookery, such as in the use of oyster and shrimp sauces. Salted and fermented black beans also impart a highly savoury taste, while ginger counteracts fishiness and garlic provides perfume.

The former British colony of Hong Kong is a magnet for world travellers and business people and its cuisine has evolved accordingly. The demand for superb food has forced local chefs to be constantly inventive and professional, developing a reputation for cutting-edge cooking. Today, many Chinese restaurants around the world take pride in promoting 'Hong Kong style' dishes, which essentially means Cantonese food with an innovative twist.

cleaver and chopping board

China's characteristic knife, the cleaver, may seem like a lethal guillotine to the uninitiated, but it is surprisingly easy to use. Its versatility as chopper, slicer, crusher, tenderiser and scooper effectively eliminates the need for a battery of knives in the kitchen. With care, a cleaver lasts more than a lifetime, and in China (as well as countries such as Singapore, Indonesia and Malaysia, where it is also used) the family knife is often passed on to the next generation.

1 Chopping board Chinese people traditionally use a block of natural, hard wood that is a complete round cut from a whole tree trunk rather than several pieces of wood fused together, as are many chopping boards today. The furious chopping action of the heavy Chinese cleaver will inevitably chip a synthetic board, but a natural wood board can absorb the blows without splintering. Cleaning such boards can be a problem. Chinese chefs use their cleavers to scrape off any embedded bits of food in order to prevent contamination. As a result, over time, the boards become slightly concave.

2, 3, 4 Cleavers Heavier than most other knives, the cleaver is honed to razor sharpness and balanced to give the leverage needed to cut through joints of meat and even bone. There are several sizes and weights, made from a variety of materials. They may have wooden handles or be cast from one single piece of metal. While the modern stainless steel models produced by Western manufacturers may look impressive, they do tend to require frequent sharpening, as do the old-fashioned iron knives sold in Chinese supermarkets. A better choice is carbonised steel, which should be wiped rather than washed after use to prevent discoloration, and given a light coat of vegetable oil to prevent rusting.

Using a cleaver

Peeling With the fingertips of one hand, hold down the piece of root vegetable firmly. Hold the cleaver in your other hand with its sharp edge positioned between the skin and the vegetable flesh. Press down firmly all the way to peel off one strip at a time. Turn the vegetable and repeat until all the skin has been peeled.

Tenderising meat Turn the cleaver over so that the blunt end is facing down. Make heavy blows all over the sliced meat, turning it over once to do the other side. When properly tenderised, the meat should have slight ruts in it and be roughly 20 per cent larger and flatter than when you started.

Scooping Tilt the cleaver at an angle, with the sharp edge pointing away from you. Run the flat side of the blade underneath the prepared food in one movement and scoop up the pieces ready to place on a serving dish, or in a bowl or wok. Lightly rest your hand on top of the food to help it onto the cleaver if necessary.

Chopping To prepare bok choy for cooking, hold the leaf of one stem lightly with one hand. Place the cleaver at a slight angle, resting the flat of the blade gently against the hand holding the bok choy. Measure the required distance from the thick edge of the stalk and press down, making clean cuts to separate leaf and stalk.

Shredding To cut fine julienne of firm ingredients such as root ginger, place the food on the cutting board and slice off the skin, removing the broadest sides first. Slice finely, keeping the food in one piece as much as possible. Then place several slices one on top of the other and cut through the layers to give fine shreds.

Crushing Bash the cloves of garlic with the broad, flat side of the blade and the skin will slide off smoothly. Apply pressure with one hand on the blade's flat side, near its blunt edge, and crush the garlic to the desired size. Rapid chopping will give you fine cuts but less garlic juice will be produced than when crushing

easy vegetable stir-fries

mushrooms with bamboo shoots

Soak 6 dried Chinese mushrooms until soft. Squeeze out the water, discard the stalks and cut into quarters. Halve 6 straw mushrooms. Cut 100 g bamboo shoots into 1cm strips. Heat 2 tbsp oil in a wok and stir-fry 1 tbsp crushed garlic for 1 minute. Add bamboo shoots and cook 2 minutes, then add mushrooms and stir-fry 1 minute. Add 2 tbsp sesame oil, 1 tbsp light soy sauce, 1 tsp pepper, 100ml water mixed with 1 tsp cornflour, and 2 tbsp Chinese wine. Bring to a boil and serve immediately.

sichuan four harmonies

Slice a large carrot diagonally, and blanch in boiling water for 2 minutes. Cut a yellow pepper into pieces the same size as the carrot. Quarter a large red onion. Fry 1 tbsp crushed garlic and 1 tsp crushed ginger in 2 tbsp oil for 1 minute. Add 1 tbsp sesame oil and the onion and stir-fry 2 minutes. Add the carrot, pepper, 16 mangetout, plus 1 tbsp light soy sauce, and stir-fry 2 minutes. Mix 100ml water with 2 tsp cornflour and add to the wok with 2 tbsp rice wine. Bring to a boil and serve as soon as sauce thickens.

beansprouts with spring onions

Wash 350 g beansprouts and drain thoroughly. Deseed 2 large green chillies and cut into julienne. Cut 4 spring onions into 5 cm lengths. Heat 2 tbsp oil in a wok and toss the spring onions in it for 30 seconds. Add the beansprouts and chillies and stir-fry over a high heat for 1 minute. Add 1 tsp salt and continue stir-frying for a further 30 seconds, then serve hot.

celery with straw mushrooms

Cut off the root end from a whole head of celery and trim off the leaves. Cut the stalks into 5 cm lengths, then into julienne. Wash and drain 150 g canned straw mushrooms. Heat 2 tbsp oil in a wok and stir-fry the celery for 1 minute. Add the straw mushrooms and continue stir-frying over a high heat for 2 minutes. Add 1 tsp salt and 2 tbsp water and stir continuously until the water comes to a quick boil. Serve immediately.

woks and their accessories

The wok has a mystical history dating back some 3000 years, yet in all that time has never changed its ingenious shape. Riding on the popularity of stir-frying as a healthy cooking method, it is now endorsed by chefs of many nationalities, and can be a best friend in the home kitchen too, serving as a deep-fryer, steamer, braiser and boiling pot, all in one pan.

1, 3 Woks Today woks come in a wide range of materials and sizes. The best are made of heavy cast iron and normally need only to be seasoned before use. New ones, however, must be filled with oil and heated through before being drained and dried. For other metals given to rusting, use a metal scouring pad to remove any traces of rust before you start cooking. Non-stick woks are not suited to rapid stir-frying as the action of the ladle may chip the pan's synthetic coating A wok made

from stainless steel will conduct heat very rapidly, so is liable to burn food too easily. Electric models are not ideal for stir-frying as they conduct heat at a rapid and uneven rate, however they are good for braising and steaming. Choosing a single or double handled wok is largely a matter of preference. One-handled versions are favoured by restaurants as they allow the chef to easily toss large quantities of ingredients during stir-frying, which aids the action of the wok ladle.

2 Wok lid Wok lids are necessary for braising, steaming and smoking; they are also used to facilitate the stir-frying process. When placed on the wok during cooking they create a flash of dense moist heat, thereby speeding up cooking.

4 Wok stand The wok's round base does not sit well on stovetops. These circular stands, typically made of iron, have four teeth strategically placed to grip the crossbars of the stove, allowing the wok to sit firmly

peking-style caramel walnuts

Although these delicious 'lacquered' nuts are best started the day before serving, they are well worth the effort. They can be served hot or cold and make a great talking point at drinks parties. Cashews can be used instead of, or as well as, walnuts if preferred.

Serves 8

Preparation time: 25 minutes, plus 2-12 hours drying

Tools	Ingredients
Pot	450 g shelled walnuts
Colander	200 g granulated sugar
Baking tray	450 ml groundnut oil
Wok	6 tbsp sesame seeds
Wire strainer	
Wire rack	

Method

1 Bring a large pan of water to the boil, add the walnuts, and simmer uncovered for 5-10 minutes, or until the water turns dark and the nuts start to turn pale. Drain and rinse the walnuts under a cold tap until the water runs clear.

2 Dry the nuts thoroughly with kitchen paper and spread them out on the baking tray. Pour the sugar evenly over them, then roll the nuts in the sugar so that they are completely coated. Place the tray in a cool place, preferably in a light breeze, and leave to dry overnight, or for a minimum of 2 hours.

3 When ready to proceed, heat the oil in the wok to a moderate heat. Divide the nuts into small batches so as not to crowd the pan. Add the first batch to the oil and cook for 2 minutes or until the sugar melts and the nuts are golden.

4 Using a wire-mesh strainer, lift the nuts from the oil and lay them on the wire rack, keeping them well separated. Sprinkle with some of the sesame seeds.

5 Repeat with the remaining walnuts and serve warm or cold. Alternatively, the caramelized nuts can be kept in a screwtop jar for up to 2 weeks.

wok cooking techniques

The wok's versatility obviates the need for a battery of utensils for different methods of cookery. However, it is helpful to have two woks, of 25 cm and 35 cm diameter. The larger one is better for holding bamboo steamers and for smoking, while the smaller can be used for deep-frying and braising. When storing, they can be stacked one in the other, thus taking up less kitchen space.

Deep-frying The wok's curvature means it demands much less oil to deep-fry than does a conventional deep-fryer. Place a draining rack on the side of the wok. Add oil to a depth of one-third and heat through. Fry only a few pieces of food at a time. When done, remove each item, holding it at an angle so that the excess oil drains away. Place on the draining rack to drain completely before transferring to a serving plate.

Tea-smoking Smoking is a slow, gentle heat process for cooking and flavouring foods that are not too thick or chunky, such as fish or thin slices of meat and poultry. Fill the wok to a depth of one-third with uncooked rice mixed with a few handfuls of barley grains. Sprinkle over 1 tbsp of black or green tea. Place the food on a double layer of foil, wrap firmly and lay it directly on the grains. Cover with the wok lid and place over a low heat for about 1 hour to smoke, opening the foil parcel for the last 30 minutes of cooking. Avoid using highly flavoured teas such as lapsang souchong for smoking.

Steaming You can steam foods in a wok simply by placing food on a dish that is resting on the steaming trivet. Choose a dish large enough to sit steadily on the trivet but allow room at the sides for easy removal. Fill the wok with water, making sure it is below the base of the dish. Bring to the boil, cover with the wok lid and allow the steam to circulate. Alternatively use a bamboo steamer of a diameter only slightly smaller than that of the wok. Ensure it sits at least 4 cm above the water level, and cover with the steamer's own lid.

Braising The technique of braising involves cooking food gently in a flavoursome liquid in a closed container. The liquid should just cover the main ingredients. The long, gentle simmering process will reduce it by about half. Open the lid occasionally during cooking to check on the evaporation rate and top up with a little liquid if necessary. When the food is cooked, remove it and reduce the gravy further by boiling vigorously until thickened, which will also intensify its flavour.

fish in chilli bean sauce

British-born writer and radio journalist fuchsia dunlop speaks fluent Mandarin and trained to be a chef in Chengdu. This dish from her highly acclaimed book *Sichuan Cookery* is one of her personal favourites, and beautifully demonstrates the region's famous love of chilli.

Serves 4
Preparation time: 30 minutes

Tools	Ingredients
Cleaver	1 whole carp, trout or grey mullet,
Chopping board	weighing about 750 g
Large dish	160 ml groundnut oil
Wok and ladle	*For the marinade*
Wok lid	¾ tsp salt
Small bowl	1-2 tbsp Shaoxing wine

For the sauce
4 tbsp Sichuanese chilli bean paste
1 tbsp finely chopped fresh ginger
1 tbsp finely chopped garlic
300 ml chicken stock
1 tsp white sugar
1-2 tsp light soy sauce
¾ tsp potato flour
½ tsp Chinkiang or black Chinese vinegar
3 spring onions, green parts only, finely sliced

Method

1 Use the cleaver to make 4 or 5 shallow diagonal cuts into each side of the fish, and pierce its head. Place in a large dish and rub the fish inside and out with the salt and Shaoxing wine. Leave to marinate while you assemble the other ingredients.

2 In the wok, heat 100 ml of oil over a high heat until smoking. Dry the fish with kitchen paper and fry it briefly on each side, just long enough to crisp up the skin. Remove and set aside. Rinse and dry the wok.

3 Return the wok to a medium heat with 4 tbsp of fresh oil. When it is hot, add the chilli bean paste and stir-fry for 20-30 seconds until the oil is red and smells delicious. Add the ginger and garlic and stir-fry for another 20 seconds or so or until you can smell their fragrance. Then pour in the stock, turn up the heat and bring the liquid to a boil. Season to taste with the sugar and soy sauce.

4 Gently place the fish in the wok and spoon some sauce over it. Turn the heat down, cover and simmer for 8-10 minutes until the fish is cooked and has absorbed some of the flavours of the sauce. Turn the fish once during cooking, spooning over some more sauce.

5 Carefully remove the cooked fish to a serving dish. In a small bowl, dissolve the potato flour in 1 tbsp cold water and add to the sauce, stirring briefly until it thickens. Throw in the vinegar and green spring onions, stir a few times, then pour the sauce over the waiting fish and serve.

braised five-spice belly pork

Originally from Northern China, this popular dish has transcended the provincial borders and is now cooked in almost every Chinese kitchen. In the north it is traditionally served with a steamed bread known as man dou, while in the south it is most commonly served with rice.

Serves 4
Preparation time: 45 minutes

Tools	Ingredients	Method
Cleaver	2 tbsp oil	**1** Heat the oil in the wok and add the sugar. Cook until the sugar caramelises and turns light brown, then add the pork slices and turn them in the mixture until they are well coated.
Chopping board	1 tbsp sugar	
Wok and ladle	500 g belly pork, sliced	
Wok lid	5 tbsp dark soy sauce	
	2 tsp five-spice powder	**2** Add the soy sauce, five-spice powder, water and salt. Cover and cook gently over a low heat for 40 minutes, turning once or twice during braising. Top up with more water if necessary.
	1 litre water	
	1 tsp salt	**3** Adjust the seasoning by adding extra soy sauce to taste, then serve.

yang zhou fried rice

Fried rice must be the best-travelled Chinese dish of all and turns up in myriad guises around the world, even though it derives from the pragmatic need to recycle leftovers. This classic version is believed to have originated in the southern province of Yang Zhou and is positively ambrosial, with lots of premium ingredients including roast pork, crab meat and prawns.

Serves 4

Preparation time: 20 minutes

Tools	Ingredients	Method
Fork	800 g cold cooked rice	1 Give the cold cooked rice a thorough raking to separate the grains. Devein the prawns, making a deep slit down the back of each one.
Cleaver	100 g raw prawns, peeled	
Chopping board	2 tbsp oil	
Wok and ladle	2 spring onions, chopped, plus extra to garnish	2 Heat the oil in the wok and fry the spring onions for 1 minute. Push them to one side of the pan.
	3 eggs	3 Crack in the eggs and cook until set. Remove from the wok and cut up roughly.
	150 g roast pork or cooked ham, diced	4 Add the rice, prawns, pork or ham, and crab meat. Stir-fry vigorously for 3 minutes.
	100 g crab meat	
	2 tbsp frozen green peas	5 Add the frozen peas, soy sauce, pepper and crumble in the stock cube. Stir-fry for 3 minutes more, then serve garnished with the extra chopped spring onion.
	2 tbsp light soy sauce	
	1 tsp black pepper	
	1 chicken stock cube	

cooking pots

While the wok reigns supreme in every Chinese kitchen, stir-frying is by no means the only cooking method. Various types of pot play important roles in the preparation of stocks, stews and braised dishes. A good stock is very important to Chinese soups, and the wok's open shape and rapid evaporation rate make it unsuitable for stock making. Pot dishes are common one-dish meals among many rural Chinese families in colder regions.

1 Stock pot Soups and stocks play important roles in Chinese cuisine, so large conventional cooking pots, much the same as those used in Western kitchens, are necessary. The most basic pot used would be a plain aluminium one, however today they are largely of modern design and made of stainless steel.

3 Double-boiler This ancient Chinese utensil is much like a French bain-marie, and used for slow simmering and stewing; this model is enamel. A single-handled lower container (for water) is fitted with a slightly smaller upper container (for the food to be cooked), which has with its own handle and a tight-fitting lid. In ancient times in China it was used strictly for herbal stews that required long, slow and gentle cooking from an indirect heat source. Today such pots are widely used in Southeast Asia for sweet coconut custards.

2 Clay or sand pots The name of these lidded pots refers to their rough exterior. They come with either one or two handles, and can be either glazed or unglazed. These pots need gentle handling, as they are delicate and crack easily under intense heat. They can be used directly on an electric ring or ceramic hotplate but not on a gas fire as this may cause cracking; using a heat diffusion mat can help to prevent this. The wire frame surrounding the pot is intended to help to protect its fragile nature. Clay pots serve as an oven-to-table utensil when food must be presented piping hot or still sizzling. The best way to do this is to cook the dish in a conventional wok and then transfer it to a clay pot that has been preheated in a very hot oven for 30 minutes. The pots come in several sizes, large enough to cradle a whole duck or small enough for one portion of stew or a braised dish. Any dish cooked in them must contain a portion of liquid. Always use a wooden spoon with clay pots, as metal will scratch the delicate interior, and lift the lid away from you when you take it off the pot in order to protect your face from the release of built-up steam.

4 Hunan pot Originating from the province of Hunan, these finely crafted, delicate clay or terracotta pots with a funnel in the centre are typically used for festive rituals. They were originally used for serving medicinal brews and herbal soups that only well-to-do families could afford. Hunan pots are not robust enough to be placed on direct heat, and so herbal soups are poured into them after being cooked in other pots.

double-boiled black chicken soup with shark's fin and sea cucumber

Black chicken is a special genus of the bird that has jet-black skin but is like any other chicken in flavour. The Chinese believe it to have rejuvenative properties. This is a popular medicinal dish from chef peter tsang of the Shang Palace at the Shangri-la Hotel in Singapore.

Serves 6

Preparation time: 3 hours 15 minutes

Tools	Ingredients
Large pot	1 black chicken
Colander	120 g sea cucumber
Cleaver	40 g ginseng
Chopping board	100 g shark's fin, soaked and boiled
Double-boiler	1 tsp salt
	½ tsp pepper
	5 red dates
	4 slices ginger

Method

1 Clean the chicken and blanch it in a pot of boiling water for 3 minutes. Drain in a colander. Meanwhile, slice the sea cucumber into 1 cm pieces and cut the ginseng into strips or slices.

2 Place the blanched chicken in the top section of a double-boiler with 1.2 litres of water. Add the sea cucumber and ginseng, plus the precooked shark's fin, salt, pepper, red dates and sliced ginger.

3 Fill the bottom section with water up to the halfway mark. Cover the top section and simmer for 3 hours over a low heat. Check periodically to make sure there is still water in the bottom section and top up if necessary.

4 Transfer to a serving dish and serve.

tung-po mutton

Su Tung-Po (1036–1101) was a poet, painter, calligrapher and epicure. A native of Sichuan, he spent most of his life travelling around China and is credited with the invention of this famous dish. This version comes from cookery author and teacher deh-ta hsiung who has written dozens of authoritative books on Chinese cuisine.

Serves 4

Preparation time: 1 hour

Tools	Ingredients
Cleaver	4 tbsp oil
Chopping board	400 g stewing mutton or lamb, cubed
Wok and ladle	2 large potatoes, cubed
Deep pot	1 large carrot, cubed
	2 tbsp dark soy sauce
	1 tbsp ginger purée
	1 tsp five-spice powder
	100 ml Chinese wine or sherry
	1 tsp sugar
	1 tsp salt
	1 litre water

Method

1 Heat the oil in a wok and fry the meat until the surfaces are sealed. Remove and set aside to drain on kitchen paper.

2 Fry the potatoes in the remaining oil until light brown. Add the carrot and fry for 2 minutes. Remove the vegetables and set aside.

3 Transfer the meat, seasonings and water to a deep pot and simmer, covered, for 40 minutes until the gravy is thick.

4 Add the potatoes and carrot and continue to cook for a further 15 minutes, then serve hot.

clay pot rice with salt fish and chicken

This traditional Cantonese dish successfully combines seafood with meat, and is redolent with ginger, garlic and sesame oil. Salt fish is much loved in China, not only as a savoury ingredient but as a fragrant salting agent, eliminating the need for additional salt. Generally, only a small amount is used and cut up into tiny pieces so that the salt flavour is well distributed in the dish.

Serves 4
Preparation time: 45 minutes

Tools	Ingredients
Clay pot	200 g jasmine rice, washed
Rice cooker	750 ml water
Cleaver	1 chicken breast
Chopping board	2 Chinese sausages
Wok and ladle	150 g salt fish fillet
	3 tbsp oil
	2 tbsp grated ginger
	3 cloves garlic, sliced
	2 tbsp sesame oil
	2 tbsp oyster sauce
	2 tbsp dark soy sauce
	1 tsp black pepper
	2 tbsp chopped spring onions

Method

1 Preheat the oven to 240°C/Gas 9 and place the clay pot in it to heat through while you cook.

2 Cook the rice in the water in the rice cooker for 12 minutes. Meanwhile, cut the chicken into 2 cm cubes, slice the sausages diagonally into pieces 0.5 cm thick, and finely dice the salt fish.

3 Heat the oil in a wok and fry the ginger and garlic until light brown. Add the chicken, sausage, fish, sesame oil, oyster sauce, dark soy sauce and pepper and toss well for 4 minutes.

4 Combine the contents of the wok with the cooked rice and transfer to the preheated clay pot. Garnish with the chopped spring onions and serve.

steamers and related tools

The culinary technique of steaming food is steeped in Yin-Yang philosophy. In China the belief is that fried foods must be counteracted by those that contain less or no oil and are therefore healthier. Steaming uses minimal amounts of flavourings, allowing the natural flavours of food to come through. It is an excellent way of cooking the seafood that is so prolific in China's coastal and inland riverine areas. Lean meats and lean poultry joints become more succulent and flavoursome when steamed, and no nutrients are lost, as they are with boiling. Last but certainly not least, steaming requires very little skill from the cook: so there are many good reasons to incorporate more steamed dishes in your culinary repertoire.

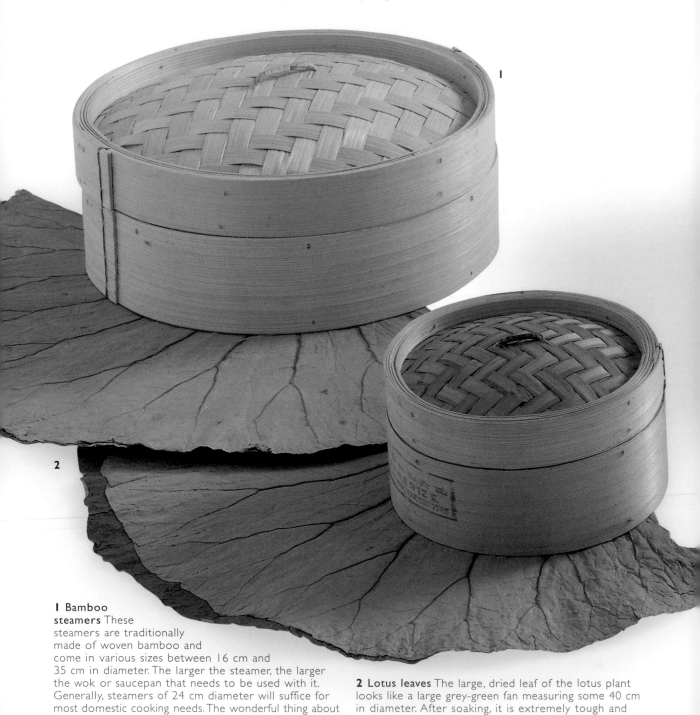

1 Bamboo steamers These steamers are traditionally made of woven bamboo and come in various sizes between 16 cm and 35 cm in diameter. The larger the steamer, the larger the wok or saucepan that needs to be used with it. Generally, steamers of 24 cm diameter will suffice for most domestic cooking needs. The wonderful thing about steamers is that you can stack them one on top of the other, and cook various foods using the same steam power. Steamers need only be rinsed in cold water and dried after being used. Never use detergents to wash bamboo steamers as they absorb cleaning agents.

2 Lotus leaves The large, dried leaf of the lotus plant looks like a large grey-green fan measuring some 40 cm in diameter. After soaking, it is extremely tough and pliable, and suitable for wrapping all kinds of foods, to which it imparts a faint floral perfume during steaming. The lotus plant is held in reverence by Buddhists and Taoists and is symbolically related to the Goddess of Mercy, Kwan Yin, who is the patron saint of seafarers

3 Aluminium steamer
This modern version of the bamboo steamer comes in multiple layers and has a high domed lid, but there is also a base section to hold water, so it can be used without a wok. Although useful for similar steaming jobs, the solid lid tends to create too much condensation, so that water drops back onto the food, resulting in an unwanted 'soup'. You can prevent this by using the aluminium steamer in conjunction with the lid of a bamboo steamer, or puncture several small holes in the metal lid to create a vent.

4 One-portion aluminum steamer A handy small steamer for cooking dim sum and reheating, this is just large enough to hold two small dumplings. Several of these little steamers can fit inside a large bamboo steamer to keep individual dim sum servings hot without letting them over-cook.

5 Little metal cups These small cups are used for steaming individual portions of savoury rice flour cakes, a popular Chinese street food. The cakes are unmouled onto plates or dried palm leaves, or eaten with a spoon straight from the cup.

6 Winter melon Looking somewhat like pale, small watermelons, winter melons are important as a 'cooling' food within the Yin-Yang philosophy that classifies foods as either cooling or heating. They are often found in restaurants specialising in Chinese traditional medicine. A favourite way to prepare them is to slice off the top then hollow out the melon in order to use the flesh as food and the shell as a dish. Filled with stock, meat and its own diced flesh, the whole melon is then steamed gently until soft, negating the use of a cooking pot. Diners scoop out the cooked flesh as well as drink the savoury soup.

glutinous rice in lotus leaf

Chinese chefs are adept at cooking glutinous rice, usually wrapped around savoury mixes and often cloaked in lotus leaves. This is known as Lor Mai Fun in Cantonese. The dried leaves are fragile and before cooking need to be soaked in water until soft so that they are pliable.

Serves 4

Preparation time: 1 hour 30 minutes

Tools	Ingredients
Bamboo steamer	400 g glutinous rice, soaked for 1 hour in cold water
Plate	*For the stuffing*
Cleaver	2 tbsp oil
Chopping board	2 cloves garlic, crushed
Wok and ladle	200 g chicken meat, diced
Lotus leaf	1 Chinese sausage, finely sliced
Flat square presser	4 Chinese mushrooms, soaked and chopped
	8 canned Chinese chestnuts
	2 tbsp light soy sauce
	2 tbsp oyster sauce
	2 tbsp sesame oil
	2 tsp salt
	1 tsp black pepper
	1 tbsp dark soy sauce
	2 tbsp chopped spring onions
	chilli sauce, to serve *(optional)*

Method

1 Steam the soaked rice for 20 minutes, then set aside.
2 Heat the oil in the wok and fry the garlic for
2 minutes. Add the chicken and Chinese sausage and
stir-fry for 5 minutes. Add all the other ingredients
and continue cooking for another 5 minutes. Sprinkle
a little water on top. Remove from the heat.
3 Soak the lotus leaf in hot water for a few minutes
then remove, wipe dry and trim off the hard stalk.
4 Spread the rice out on the lotus leaf to a thickness

of about 1 cm thick and use the presser to firm it up.
5 Pile the fried ingredients in the centre (top picture).
6 Lift up two opposite sides of the lotus leaf, line them
up together, and fold them over and over (bottom left).
7 Gather the remaining sides and fold them so that
the edges tuck in and under (bottom right).
8 Pat firmly and turn over, so that the seam-side is
underneath. Place on a plate in a bamboo steamer.
9 Cover and steam for 10 minutes. Unwrap and serve
straight from the leaf with chilli sauce to accompany.

steamed winter melon soup

Winter melons are about the size of footballs, and often used as a cooking pot as well as a type of bowl brought to the table. The ingredients of this nourishing soup are all contained within the scooped out melon, and the soft melon meat should be eaten as well as the soup.

Serves 6
Preparation time: 1 hour

Method

1 Bring the water to a boil in the pot and simmer the barley for 15 minutes. Meanwhile, cut off the top third of the melon and reserve it to use as a lid. Discard the pith and seeds from the shell, and scoop out the melon flesh leaving a rim of about 2.5 cm thickness all the way around the inside of the shell.

2 Add the chicken, ham and lotus seeds to the simmering barley and continue cooking for a further 15 minutes.

3 Transfer all the contents of the pot to the melon shell and add the salt and sugar. Carefully sit the melon on a plate in the steamer. Replace the melon's top and cover the steamer tightly. Cook for 30 minutes, then bring the whole melon to the table, with a few finely sliced spring onions sprinkled over the soup if desired.

Tools	Ingredients
Large pot	1 litre water
Cleaver	100 g pearl barley
Chopping board	200 g chicken breast, cubed
Whole winter melon	100 g cooked or Chinese ham, diced
Spoon	150 g canned lotus seeds, drained
Bamboo steamer with high-domed lid	2 tsp salt
	1 tsp sugar
	finely sliced spring onion, to garnish

small cooking utensils

While Chinese kitchens are not cluttered with equipment, there are a number of small tools that can be very handy for specific jobs. On occasions when you feel the urge to make special dishes and snacks like sweet tofu, home-made noodles, and steamed or fried vegetable cakes, these tools help to make the job a cinch.

1 Stock scoop Good stock base (especially chicken stock) is essential to China's large variety of soups. This small aluminium bucket on a long handle is used to ladle the prepared stock from large, deep pots.

2, 4 Tofu scoops A plain round piece of metal, with or without a handle, serves as a scoop for tofu when portions need to be cut from a large slab. Commonly used in factories, they are also employed by Chinese street food vendors who scoop out individual portions of sweet tofu for their customers.

3 Flat square presser This aluminium square with handle is used to press down steamed cakes made from mashed radish or yam to prevent air bubbles forming during cooking.

5 Thread noodle slicer Noodles are fundamental to Chinese cuisines, and are most commonly made with wheat or rice flour, though bean thread vermicelli or cellophane noodles, made from mung bean starch, are also popular. Making fresh noodles at home in small quantities is relatively easy (in fact, it is very similar to pastry or pasta making) and the results taste much better than store-bought noodles. Chinese noodle makers make their noodles from rolled-out sheets of dough and cut them to varying widths with this tool – wider ribbons for soups, thinner for stir-fries. The slicer, a broad stainless steel blade measuring about 12.5 cm x 7.5 cm, is attached to a wooden handle and is used to cut and scoop up the strands of raw noodle dough.

dim sum utensils

The phrase dim sum means 'food to touch the heart', and the range of dim sum foods is endless, especially when you consider that every regional Chinese cuisine has its own favoured recipes. There are, however, specific types of dim sum dish, including fried, steamed, savoury and sweet, plus a small range of rice-based dishes such as congee with century egg, salt fish or chicken.

1 Cup cake moulds Popular Chinese street food items, such as Chui Kueh (water cakes) or Little Buddhas (steamed rice cakes with a savoury radish mixture), are made in these small aluminium cups.

2 Jelly and tart moulds These come in aluminium or plastic, with simple scalloped patterns or pineapple, fish, turtle and rabbit motifs. Each motif is symbolic: pineapple for nobility (in Chinese the word sounds the same as that for emperor); fish for rebirth; rabbit for wisdom; and turtle for longevity.

3 Reeded pastry brush Thin pieces of bamboo are fused together to make an easy-to-grasp handle for this broad, fine-haired brush which is as functional as it is beautiful. It can be used for egg-washing, basting tarts and other festive cakes, as well as lightly dusting things with flour.

4 Won ton spreader A thin, short piece of finely honed wood is used to scoop up and spread small amounts of minced pork or seafood when making won ton dumplings. The flat shape ensures that just enough of the filling mixture is placed on the won ton skins.

5 Dumpling dough roller This tool is much smaller and thinner than a conventional rolling pin, and fits nicely into the palm of one hand, leaving the other free to manipulate the dumpling dough when rolling it out. The roller is made of light wood and is about 25 cm long.

mushroom and leek spring rolls

A long sojourn in France inspired esteemed American chef ming tsai of the Blue Ginger restaurant in Boston to devise this recipe, which uses leeks to give a French twist to traditional Chinese spring rolls. They make excellent party canapés.

Serves 4-6

Preparation time: 1 hour

Tools	Ingredients
Cleaver	75 g cellophane noodles
Chopping board	2 tbsp oil, plus extra for deep-frying
Vegetable shredder	1 tbsp finely chopped garlic
Medium bowl	1 tbsp finely chopped root ginger
Strainer or large sieve	2 serrano chillies, finely chopped
Wok and ladle	125 ml hoisin sauce
Large spoon	125 g shiitake mushroom caps, thinly sliced
Wire mesh ladle	2 large leeks, white parts only, julienned
	8 tbsp chopped fresh coriander
	100 g spring onions, chopped
	16 spring roll wrappers, about 20 cm square
	1 egg, beaten with 4 tbsp water
	salt and pepper

Method

1 Soak the cellophane noodles in a bowl of hot water for 10-15 minutes or until soft. Drain thoroughly, then chop them into pieces 5 cm long.

2 Heat the wok over a high heat. Add the oil and swirl to coat the pan. When the oil is hot, add the garlic, ginger and chillies and cook until soft, about 2 minutes. Do not allow the aromatics to burn.

3 Reduce the heat to medium, add the hoisin sauce, and cook until it loses its raw taste, about 3 minutes. Add the shiitake mushrooms and leeks and cook until soft, about 6 minutes. Season with salt and pepper.

4 Transfer the filling mixture to a strainer, and with a large spoon, press the mixture well to drain it thoroughly. Leave to cool.

5 Transfer the filling mixture to a medium bowl and add the coriander, spring onions and softened cellophane noodles. Stir to blend.

6 Dampen a kitchen towel. Place 5 wrappers on a work surface with 1 point of each near you, and cover the remainder with the cloth to prevent drying.

7 Place about 4 tbsp of the filling on the wrappers just above the near corners. Bring the corner nearest you up over the filling and roll halfway. Fold in the side corners, brush the edges with egg wash, then continue rolling to enclose the filling completely, rolling as tightly as possible. Cover with the cloth and allow the rolls to rest, seam side down. Fill and roll the remaining wrappers, cover, and allow to rest at least 2 minutes.

8 Fill the cleaned wok one-third full with oil and heat to 180°C over a high heat. Working in batches, fry the spring rolls until golden, turning as needed, for about 5 minutes. Remove with a wire mesh ladle and drain on paper towels. Slice the rolls on the diagonal or in half and serve hot with a dipping sauce.

making potstickers

These delightful dumplings, known as potstickers in China, are a relative of the Japanese gyoza. The pastry is rolled out as thinly as possible, but not so thinly that the potstickers break when fried, as the crimped and pleated edges look nicer when the pastry is delicate.

shanghai pork dumplings

The traditional method of cooking potstickers is to fry them until their bases are brown, literally 'sticking' to the pan, hence the name. A little water is then added to flash-steam the dumplings until they are fully cooked, but be careful as it will splatter on hitting the oil.

Serves 6

Preparation time: 45 minutes

Tools	Ingredients
Cleaver	100 g spring
Chopping board	onions
Mixing bowl	300 g pork mince
Small rolling pin	1 tsp salt
Won ton	1 tsp black
spreader	pepper
Lidded frying pan	2 tbsp sesame oil
Wok ladle	1 tbsp cornflour
	24 dumpling skins
	oil for frying

Method

1 Finely chop the spring onions and place in a mixing bowl with the pork mince. Add the salt, pepper, sesame oil and cornflour and blend thoroughly so that the seasoning is well incorporated.

2 Using a won ton spreader, place a good dollop of mixture onto the centre of a dumpling skin (top left). Dab around the edge of the skin with a little water (top centre). Fold the skin over to make a half moon shape, and seal sides firmly with the thumb and forefinger (top right).

3 Holding the sealed edge with both hands, make a pleat one side of the dumpling (bottom left). Repeat to give 2 or 3 folds much like the ruffle on a curtain (bottom centre). Press down gently on the pleats so that they stay in shape (bottom right). Repeat with the remaining won ton wrappers and mince mixture.

4 Heat a frying pan with a little oil and place about 6 of the dumplings in it bottom-side down, pressing a little so that they sit firmly. Fry the dumplings until the bases are brown.

5 Add about 2 tbsp of water to the pan, then quickly cover with a lid and steam-cook the dumplings until the pan is dry. Serve them hot with a dipping sauce of black vinegar and shredded ginger.

moist, tender dough of exquisite thinness
encloses a juicy mince of seasoned pork and spring
onions, pan-fried to golden richness

steamed prawn shao mai

Shao mai is just one of hundreds of items within the dim sum range. These delicate pea-topped dumplings are filled with savoury prawn mince flavoured simply with ginger, garlic, spring onions and sesame oil. Won ton skins or 'wrappers' are available ready-made from Chinese grocers.

Serves 4
Preparation time: 30 minutes

Tools	Ingredients
Cleaver	500 g raw tiger prawns, shelled
Chopping board	1 tbsp garlic purée
Mixing bowl	1 tbsp ginger purée
Steaming plate	2 tbsp sesame oil
Won ton spreader	1 tsp black pepper
Bamboo steamer	1 tbsp cornflour
Wok	1 egg, lightly beaten
	1 tsp salt
	1 tbsp light soy sauce
	2 spring onions, finely chopped
	20-30 won ton skins
	30 large frozen garden peas

Method

1 Mince the prawns with a cleaver until their texture resembles chopped nuts. Place in a mixing bowl with the garlic, ginger, sesame oil, pepper and cornflour and stir well. Add the beaten egg, salt, soy sauce and spring onions and mix thoroughly.

2 Using the won ton spreader, place a good dollop of filling onto a won ton skin (top). Then draw the sides up and shape into a little straight-sided dumpling (bottom). Trim off the ends of the won ton skin so that the edge of the skin is flush with the filling. Place a single green pea in the centre. Repeat with the remaining mixture and won ton skins.

3 Place the shao mai on a lightly oiled steaming plate, making sure they do not touch. Fill the base of the steamer with water and bring to the boil. Place the plate in the steamer, cover and cook for 20 minutes.

barbecued pork buns

This star item is a dim sum classic, a fluffy, light dough encasing savoury-sweet roast pork, or sometimes chicken. The same dough can be used for sweet buns, made simply by placing a spoonful of mashed red beans, sold canned in all Chinese stores, in the centre of the dough.

Serves 4

Preparation time: 45 minutes, plus 2 hours rising time

Method

1 To make the dough, dissolve the sugar in the warm water and sprinkle the yeast over. Stir and leave for 15 minutes in a warm spot until a froth begins to form.

2 Sift the flour and salt into a large bowl. Add the yeast mixture and mix to a dough. Knead on a floured board for 15 minutes or until the dough is elastic and smooth.

3 Place the dough in a warm, dry bowl and leave to rise in a warm spot for about 2 hours.

4 To make the filling, cut the pork into thick strips and marinate in the hoi sin sauce, wine and sugar for 10 minutes. Preheat the oven to 200°C/Gas 6.

5 Place the pork on a rack in a roasting pan and roast in the oven for 35 minutes. Leave to cool, then cut into 1 cm dice.

6 Shape the dough into a cylinder of 5 cm in diameter. Cut into rounds 1 cm thick, then roll each into a thin circle 8 cm in diameter. Place 1 tbsp of roast pork in the centre of a circle, then bring up the sides of the dough and pinch to seal firmly. Repeat with the remaining circles of dough.

7 Prepare a steamer by filling the base with water and bringing it to a boil. Cut several squares of grease-proof paper the size of the base of the dumplings. Oil the paper lightly and place a dumpling on each square. Sit the dumplings in the steamer, cover and cook for 20 minutes. Serve hot or at room temperature.

Tools	Ingredients
Cleaver	*For the dough*
Chopping board	1 tsp sugar
Mixing bowl	250 ml warm water
Fine sieve	2 tsp dried yeast
Small spoon	450 g plain flour
Steamer and lid	a pinch of salt
Wok	*For the barbecued pork filling*
Roasting pan with rack	250 g rib cut pork
Pastry brush	2 tbsp hoi sin sauce
	2 tbsp Chinese wine
	1 tsp sugar

serving utensils

Unlike in a formal Western meal where the types of crockery and cutlery depend on the kind of food on the menu, a Chinese table is relatively simple and constant whatever is served. Chinese meals are generally communal in nature, with a selection of different dishes served all at once, with or without a central bowl of soup. Diners have their individual set of rice bowl, chopsticks and porcelain spoon and simply help themselves from the dishes available.

1 Teapot Tea is the favourite accompaniment to food in Chinese restaurants, although contrary to popular belief, it is rarely served with food in Chinese homes. The tea leaves are placed in the pot and hot water added again and again as needed. The traditional shape of Chinese teapots is round and squat, though they are taking on other shapes as fashion changes.

2 Tea cups Tea is served in small cups and replenished often. When offered in the home as refreshment to guests, the tea is presented with both hands and drunk likewise, hence the absence of saucers and handles.

3 Porcelain rice bowl The shape and size of traditional Chinese rice bowls have remained unchanged for centuries. To hold the bowl, place your thumb on the upper rim and four fingers on the lower rim. The bowl

is supposed to be held near the mouth and rice delicately pushed in with chopsticks. Rice is not meant to be picked up a few grains at a time, as in China the grains dropping between the chopsticks denote bad luck.

4 Soup noodle bowl Noodles are meant to be one-dish meals in themselves and large bowls such as this are used for serving soup-based noodle dishes.

5 Small sauce dishes These come in various sizes and shapes, some compartmentalised so that they can contain a few items such as soy sauce, grated ginger, chilli sauce, sliced chillies, mustard or vinegar.

6 Dinner plate The Chinese do not serve rice on a plate, except as a token gesture to Westerners who are not used to eating rice from a bowl. Plates such as this one are used only when a one-dish meal is served, for example fried noodles. However, such plates are commonly used in Southeast Asia and Indochina.

7 Soup bowl The traditional family mode of eating soup is for all diners to dip into a large, central bowl for repeated mouthfuls. Today, individual soup bowls such as this are a common sight, owing to modern hygiene requirements. Individual portions of congee are also served in this type of bowl.

8, 9 Porcelain spoon and rest As porcelain conducts heat badly, these are sensible implements for drinking hot soup without scalding the lips, as the spoon remains cool. Such spoons are also used for mixing and stirring sauces and marinades that contain vinegar, as a metal spoon can react with acidic ingredients. The spoon rest prevents stains being made on the tablecloth.

10 Chopsticks rest The porcelain chopstick rest helps to keep the food-stained tips of the chopsticks off the tablecloth, and decorated versions are one of the formal touches to be expected at banquets.

11 Chopsticks Normal chopsticks for eating are about 24 cm long, and are traditionally made from bamboo or wood. In ancient China, imperial classes used ivory or even solid gold. Plastic chopsticks are not ideal for eating noodles, as they are slippery. Lacquer chopsticks are intended for ornamental use rather than eating but can be used for cold dishes.

12 Soup tureen A soup tureen is generally used for serving soup at the centre of the table. It also makes an ideal serving container for stews. The lid keeps heat in effectively. There are no handles and it is important to wear kitchen gloves when moving the hot tureen.

13 Soup ladle A large porcelain ladle such as this is used to serve soups from tureens. It normally features a slightly curved handle and flat-bottomed bowl section.

14 Soy sauce bottle The Chinese equivalent of the Western salt and pepper cruet, the soy sauce bottle is typical of restaurant rather than home use. It is placed on the dining table for individual seasoning of meals. However, in a Chinese home, any extra sauce is meant as a dip and presented in small dishes for shared use.

how to use chopsticks

Whether made of wood, bamboo or classy silver, chopsticks can be exasperating for those not familiar with their use. However, they can be mastered and with a little practice at holding and clicking them together, it will soon be easy to pick up even the tiniest, slipperiest morsels.

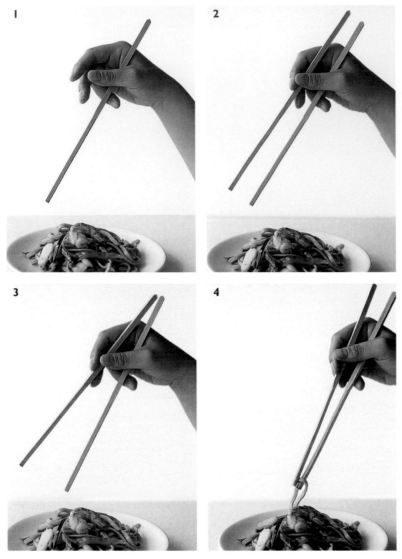

Beginners will find bamboo or wooden chopsticks easier to use than plastic, and square-cut Chinese chopsticks easier to handle than pointed Japanese models. Practise clicking the chopsticks together before moving on to pick up food with them. The most important thing to remember is that only the top chopstick should move.

Step 1 Grasp one chopstick about a third of the way along, between the base of the thumb and the tip of the third finger. This chopstick must be kept steady throughout use. Some people (especially children) find it easier to hold chopsticks about halfway along, but hold them too far back or forwards and they will not provide enough leverage, and will be unwieldy to use.

Step 2 Hold the second chopstick between the tips of the thumb, first and seconds fingers, holding it above the other chopstick, again about a third of the way along. When the chopsticks are held parallel to each other, there should be a space of about 2 cm between them.

Step 3 Keeping your thumb as the anchor, use the tip of your second finger to raise the front of the top chopstick, thus opening the set.

Step 4 Maintain control by keeping the bottom chopstick steady, and use your second finger to lower the top chopstick, bringing the tips together with a light pressure so that you can grasp a piece of food.

hot and sour prawn lo mein

Method

1 Peel, devein and rinse the prawns and set aside. Bring a small pan of water to the boil and blanch the water chestnuts for 10 seconds, then refresh under cold water, drain and pat dry.

2 Bring a large pot of water to the boil, add the noodles and cook until they are just tender. Rinse under cold water in the colander, and set aside to drain thoroughly.

3 To make the ginger marinade, combine the Chinese rice wine, ginger, and sesame oil in a bowl. Add the prawns, toss lightly to coat and set aside. To make the hot and sour sauce, in a separate bowl, mix together the stock, soy sauce, Chinese rice wine, sugar, vinegar, sesame oil and cornflour, then set aside.

4 Heat a wok over a high heat. Add 2 tbsp of the oil and heat until very hot but not smoking. Lift the prawns from the marinade and add them to the wok. Toss lightly for about 1½ minutes until they turn pink. Remove with a handled strainer and drain in a colander. Wipe out the wok.

5 Reheat the wok over a medium-high heat. Add the remaining 1½ tbsp of oil and heat for about 20 seconds or until hot. Add the onion, garlic and chilli paste and stir-fry until the onion is slightly softened, 1½-2 minutes.

6 Add the water chestnuts and mangetout, turn up the heat to high, and toss until heated through. Add the hot and sour sauce and cook, stirring constantly to prevent lumps, until the sauce is thickened, 2-3 minutes.

7 Add the prawns and noodles and mix gently. Transfer to a platter and serve immediately

hot and sour prawn lo mein

'When I was growing up, "ordering Chinese" invariably meant lo mein noodles,' says US culinary expert nina simonds. 'The Cantonese lo mein I loved as a child, however, bears little resemblance to this bright, fresh-tasting and virtually greaseless version. Whenever I'm feeling nostalgic, I toss noodles in this spicy sauce laced with garlic, vinegar and hot chillies.'

Serves 6
Preparation time: 30 minutes

Tools	Ingredients
Cleaver	700 g medium-sized raw prawns
Chopping board	175 g canned water chestnuts, drained and sliced
Small pot	225 g wide flat noodles
Large pot	3½ tbsp oil
Colander	1 medium red onion, thinly sliced
Small bowls	2½ tbsp finely chopped garlic
Wok and ladle	1 tsp hot chilli paste
Wire mesh	225 g mangetout, ends snapped and strings removed
strainer	*For the ginger marinade*
	3 tbsp Chinese rice wine or sake
	1½ tbsp finely chopped fresh ginger
	1 tsp sesame oil
	For the hot and sour sauce
	340 ml Chinese chicken stock or water
	5½ tbsp soy sauce
	2 tbsp Chinese rice wine or sake
	2 tbsp sugar
	2 tbsp Chinese black vinegar or Worcestershire sauce
	1 tsp toasted sesame oil
	1 tbsp cornflour

soup and congee

Most Chinese people have a penchant for soups, derived from the Yin-Yang philosophy that they are sustaining because their ratio of substance to liquid is purported to right any bodily imbalance. The variety of soups is wide. Some are practically stews with lots of meat, seafood or noodles and meant as complete meals in themselves. Lighter soups have a different role to play as refreshing dishes, or to help dry dishes go down well. Congee is a rice porridge, the staple of most rural communities in South China, and typical breakfast fare. Traditionally it is made with broken rice grains. For variety, the basic mixture can be flavoured with a wide range of tasty extras such as white fish, shredded chicken, mushrooms, dough sticks, fresh coriander and sliced chillies.

chicken and mushroom
soup Cut 1 chicken breast into 1 cm cubes. Wash 250 g mushrooms under a cold tap and cut into bite-sized pieces. Place the mushrooms and chicken in a pot with 800 ml water, 1 chicken stock cube and 1 tbsp light soy sauce. Bring to the boil and simmer for 25 minutes. Add 1 tbsp chopped parsley and ½ tsp ground black pepper, then serve hot.

congee with shrimp and spring onions
Wash thoroughly 200 g jasmine rice and place in a pot with 1.5 litres water. Bring to the boil, cover and simmer for 40 minutes until the rice grains are slightly pulpy and the surrounding liquid is opaque white. Shell and clean 150 g small raw prawns. Add them to the congee and simmer for 5 minutes. In the last minute, add 1 tbsp sesame oil and ½ tsp pepper. Garnish the congee with 2 tbsp finely chopped spring onions just before serving.

japan
and
korea

japan and korea

Japanese culture may be difficult for non-Japanese to fathom because of its near-mystical symbolism. However the genius of Japanese cooking is its simplicity, the marrying of a few flavourings with the natural goodness of fresh ingredients, and each dish a manifestation of the Japanese love of nature.

The objective of Japanese cooking is to let each ingredient, and each dish, reveal its own particular beauty and flavour. This may be in the use of an autumn leaf to garnish, an artfully arranged pickle, or the rustic colours of carefully selected china and lacquer serving dishes. It is this very simplicity that makes Japanese cuisine so wonderfully enchanting. It imparts an almost Zen-like karma, with the focus not on quantity but on the reverent essence of each morsel. The Japanese eat not only with their mouths but with their souls, as witnessed when you see people contemplating every mouthful as though it were poetry.

The key flavourings used in Japanese cuisine are essentially simple. They include dashi (a stock flavoured with fish flakes and seaweed), bonito (dried fish), sake, plus soy bean products such as soy sauces and hundreds of different types of yeasty miso paste. Other common Japanese ingredients are bamboo shoots, daikon (a large white radish also known as mooli), ginger, shiitake mushrooms, nori seaweed sheets, shirataki noodles, and soba (buckwheat) noodles. Perhaps the most memorable thing for first-timers is wasabi paste, an extremely pungent condiment of green horseradish that literally 'gets up your nose'.

There are seven main types of cooking methods used in Japan. A typical meal will consist of a selection of small dishes, often three dishes each made by a different cooking method, plus miso soup, rice and pickles. Grilled dishes are known as yakimono and familiar to many Westerners as yakitori and teriyaki. Agemono are deep-fried foods such as tempura. Nimono are simmered or poached foods – essentially the stews of Japanese cooking. Mushimono are steamed items, itamemono are sautéed or pan-fried, sunomono are vinegared, and aemono are dressed dishes often featuring a substantial sauce.

The Japanese insist on serving foods in tandem with the seasons. The best Japanese restaurants maintain separate sets of dishes and serving utensils for each season. The pattern of waitresses' kimonos and sashes reflects the season – red for autumn, white for winter, green for spring and orange for summer.

The ambience will harmonise with the dishes served and food will be arranged to reflect the shapes, colours and textures of the seasons.

It is sushi that perhaps most captures Western imagination. Frequently confused with sashimi, which is simply raw fish, sushi is cooled sticky rice that has

ABOVE: 1 sushi rice, 2 kombu seaweed, 3 bonito powder, 4 hijiki seaweed, 5 seven spices chilli, 6 red pepper chilli, 7 wakame seaweed, 8 nori seaweed, 9 udon noodles, 10 sesame seeds, 11 soba noodles, 12 black sesame seeds.
OPPOSITE: 1 daikon radish, 2 shimeji mushrooms, 3 shiso leaves, 4 spinach, 5 enoki mushrooms, 6 shiitake mushrooms, 7 edamame, 8 burdock root.

been flavoured with vinegar, often topped with pieces of raw fish or shellfish and either eaten as starters or as the main focus of a meal. Japanese consider raw fish to be the high point of a meal and all dishes that follow are merely co-stars. Sushi is an art form in itself, but does not have to be purist. Nor does it have to feature raw fish.

Up until the end of the 16th century, the island nation of Japan was almost completely isolated from the rest of the world. The first Europeans to reach her shores were Portuguese seamen and in their wake, trade between the two countries began in earnest. Jesuit missionaries began arriving, hoping to convert the Japanese to Christianity. They also noticed that the Japanese consumed practically no meat and ate large quantities of rice and seafood. The Portuguese began to interfere with the Japanese feudal system. This, coupled with fear of an invasion by Spaniards based in the Philippines, lead to them being forcibly expelled in 1638. All foreigners were banned and all Japanese were forbidden to leave the country on pain of death. Once more, Japan's doors were locked against the world, until the arrival of Commodore Perry in the 19th century.

What the Portuguese left behind were their recipes for deep-fried foods that came to be known as tempura. The word itself was the result of the Portuguese Catholics' rejection of meat on Ember Days, which they called by the Latin name of Quatuor Tempora, the 'four times' of the year. They asked instead for seafood, usually shrimp. Eventually, the name tempura became attached to the fried shrimp

BELOW: **1** kimchee yangnyum, **2** umeboshi plums, **3** gochugang chilli paste, **4** miso, **5** fried beancurd, **6** soy sauce, **7** mirin, **8** fresh tofu, **9** pickled daikon, **10** brown vinegar.

and it remains to this day, although other foods such as salmon, tofu, bamboo shoots and vegetables are also cooked in the tempura style.

Korea is a peninsula with a friendly subtemperate climate that yields abundant produce so for centuries, Koreans have eaten the products of the sea,

the land and the mountains. Korean cuisine is fragrantly spicy and hearty with basic seasonings coming from garlic, ginger, black pepper, spring onions, soy sauce and sesame seeds. Chillies are used liberally, bean paste, mustard, vinegar and rice wine also feature. The permutations of these ingredients in marinades and seasonings are endless.

No Korean person could be without kimchee, the country's spicy pickled cabbage, for more than a few days, and there are many versions of it. Often two or three varieties of kimchee are served as part of a meal. The pickling liquid is a blend of salt, chilli powder, fresh red chillies, ginger, soy sauce and sugar. Layer upon layer of sliced cabbage is placed in a stone jar, covered with several pieces of muslin to allow the pickle to 'breathe' and after about a week, the jar is opened to reveal an intoxicating dish.

Beef is the favourite meat in Korea and most frequently turns up as bulgogi (chilli beefsteak) or bulgabi (barbecued short ribs). It is the sauce that distinguishes these two national favourites. Yangyum kanjang is a pungent mix of soy sauce, sesame oil, bean paste, wine, spring onions, chilli paste, garlic and sugar. The steak and ribs are marinated in this paste for several hours and then grilled over hot coals or cooked on a cast-iron griddle at the table.

The Koreans often use a fermented soy bean paste similar to the Sichuan chilli bean paste. Known as gochujang, it has a surprisingly mellow flavour given the amount of ground chilli in it. Seaweed is used in many different ways, the Korean kim being similar to Japanese nori and used in much the same way, as a wrapper, or shredded and added to soups.

Korea has some unique noodles in the form of naengmyun, a rubbery buckwheat noodle made so long that the dried strands are folded in half, and when cooked are cut with scissors at the table. The name means 'cold noodle' and, while they can be served hot, they are most frequently featured floating in a cold broth.

In history, poor farming families ate a diet of boiled rice and vegetables, often eking out their supply of rice with the addition of other grains and pulses. The vegetables would be stir-fried with a sharp seasoning such as chilli and bean paste during winter, and served raw and cold in summer. The Korean diet has changed much over the past few decades and with more Koreans travelling abroad, as well as foreigners visiting the country, taste buds are being shaped by the introduction of international foods.

knives and chopping board

Top quality Japanese kitchen knives are truly the razor-sharp progeny of the Samurai fighting sword and are among the most prized possessions in Japanese homes. Forgers of these blades are regarded as living national treasures. Japanese knives are forged so that only one side of the blade holds the cutting edge, usually on the right, so that they cut much faster and more cleanly than the double-edged knives typical of Western manufacturers. Two materials are favoured: carbon steel and stainless steel. Carbon steel is superior and honed so sharply that it can literally split a hair. Always hold a Japanese knife lightly, not with a stranglehold. With the correct movement and rhythm, a knife is an extension of your hand and there should be no awkward tension while cutting.

1 Kitchen carver Known as a deba, this functions like a Chinese cleaver but is narrower and lighter, usually measuring 18 cm long and 4 cm wide. It is basically a fish knife, used for deheading, tailing and boning, but can also be used for poultry and meat. Indeed, there is no reason why this versatile implement cannot be used for other jobs, including heavy chopping work.

2 Fish slicer Traditionally used for sashimi, this long, slender knife with blunt end is known as a tacobiki, or octopus knife. It is ideal for slicing fish fillets, as well as cutting neat sushi rolls. Another type of sashimi knife, the yanagi-ba or willow-leaf blade, is also long and slender, but looks more like a Western knife as the blade ends in a fine point. Serrated knives will never do for fish slicing as they tear instead of making clean cuts. Always have a folded wet cloth close by, and frequently wipe the blade to keep it clean while working.

3 Vegetable knife Shaped and weighted like a Chinese cleaver, albeit narrower, this is used mainly for vegetable cutting but its weight and leverage make it suitable for delicate cutting, chopping and fine slicing, even bashing garlic. Choose brands made of carbon steel.

4 All-purpose knife With its 24 cm single-sided blade, this knife is a Japanese version of an all-purpose chef's knife and known as an oroshi. It can be used for preparing fish, beef, poultry and vegetables. Like the others shown here, it has a non-slip wooden handle and should be sharpened on a whetstone.

5 Chopping board The Japanese use conventional chopping boards but chefs have a preference for square or rectangular shapes made of pine. Since the cuisine relies heavily on cutting, these tend to be larger than those chopping boards normally seen in the West.

simple japanese pickles

Traditionally, Japanese pickles are much more than condiments. The art known as 'tsukemono' is actually a very extensive domain, each accompaniment regarded with the same reverence as the main course. For centuries, every home in Japan has had its own pickling crock or barrel. Pickles are relished for their piquant, salty flavours that juxtapose artfully with raw fish and unseasoned meats. They also have a sharp, cleansing effect on the palate and aid digestion.

radish pickle Finely grate I large daikon into a mixing bowl. Sprinkle 2 tsp salt all over the radish strands and stir well. Leave to stand for 20 minutes, then squeeze out as much moisture from the daikon as possible. Add 2 tbsp rice wine, I tbsp sugar and I tsp sesame seeds and toss well.

aubergine pickle Wash and dry 4 baby aubergines and cut into quarters lengthways. Rub with I tbsp salt and set aside on a piece of absorbent paper for at least I hour. Combine 150 g miso paste, 2 tbsp mirin and I tbsp finely grated ginger in a small bowl. Gently squeeze out the moisture from the aubergine and place in a shallow bowl. Pour the pickling liquid over it, cover and steep overnight or for several days. Serve with grilled fish or chicken.

turnip pickle Peel 500 g large turnips, then rinse and cut into thin julienne. Place in a bowl and sprinkle liberally with 2 tbsp salt. Set aside for 10 minutes, then squeeze out the moisture from the turnip. Add I tbsp kombu strips and I tbsp grated lemon zest and leave to stand for 30 minutes at room temperature. To serve, drain off any excess liquid and arrange in a mound next to fish or meat dishes.

sashimi

It is imperative that fish for sashimi be impeccably fresh. Place your fillet on a cutting board and hold the sashimi knife so that the blade is inclined slightly to the left. With a sweeping motion, draw the knife towards you from its base to the tip, applying gentle pressure but letting the weight of the knife do the work. Move the tip of the knife with the fish slice attached a little to one side and lay the slice on its side. Serve with shredded daikon, shiso leaves and wasabi.

sushi equipment

While many people associate sushi with raw fish, the term actually means 'vinegared rice' and consequently the rice preparation is the most important element. Having the proper tools makes all the difference to the results. The rice has to be cooled to the right temperature, and it must have the correct texture and sheen. Natural materials, such as bamboo and wood, have a special quality that ensures that the rice comes out perfect because, unlike metal, they do not react chemically with foods. Furthermore, it is virtually impossible to get the precise shape required for rolled sushi without using a genuine sushi mat.

1 Rice cooling tub Known as a hangiri, this is made from the wood of a special cypress tree and bound with copper hoops. Perfect for rapid cooling of sushi rice (which always has to be freshly made), the wood also helps give the rice its proper gloss and malleable texture. This cooling process is hastened by the use of the fan to drive off moisture and create the right flavour.

2 Wooden spatula Far from being an arcane kitchen tool, this flat, round-ended spatula is regarded as an important symbol of the Japanese housewife's domain. Usually made of wood, but sometimes decorative porcelain, it is used to turn and spread sushi rice. The wood imparts a faint flavour to the rice.

3 Fan Usually made of bamboo ribs covered with either paper or silk, fans are used to cool rice for sushi and coax glowing embers from charcoal fires.

4 Bamboo mat This 25 cm square-shaped mat of fine bamboo is for forming and pressing rice and other soft foods into cylindrical shapes. Nori sheets are toasted and placed directly on the mat and warm rice is heaped on top and flattened. The mat is then rolled up and over to make perfect sushi rolls. To avoid musty smells, wash the mat in tepid water after use, then wipe and allow to dry completely before storing.

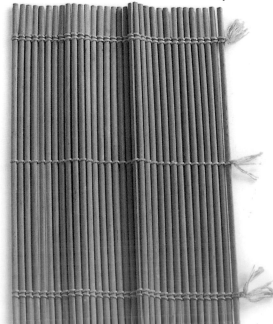

the cool softness of sticky rice, the crunch of nori seaweed
and sesame seeds, the tang of pickled ginger,
the heat of wasabi: sushi is a perfectly balanced snack

sushi techniques

Sticky rice is, as the name says, sticky. This can make it seem difficult to work with your hands, as the grains stick to your fingers. The Japanese solution is to keep a bowl of acidulated water nearby, and to dip the hands in it before picking up the rice. To make this 'hand vinegar', use 2 tbsp of rice vinegar per 125ml of water.

rolling norimaki

Toasting nori seaweed over a gas flame darkens it and makes it more pliable for rolling.

Method

1 Place the bamboo mat on a dry chopping board and lay the toasted nori on top. Add 2-3 tbsp of the cooked vinegared rice and gently spread it out over the nori until the layer of rice is thin. Leave a gap of 1.5 cm around the edge of the rice. Fill as desired.
2 Pick up the bamboo mat at the near side and roll it over to meet the other side, enclosing the rice in the nori and ensuring that the filling is at the centre of the roll.
3 Lift the bamboo mat a little, then press it gently down and over the cylinder. Roll the cylinder in the mat a little to help the sushi firm up. Pat both ends in firmly and trim away the excess seaweed.
4 Lay the nori roll on the cutting board, seam-side down. Using a sharp knife, cut into 3 cm pieces.

rolling uramaki

Also known as inside-out sushi, uramaki are a pretty alternative to norimaki and have the crunch and nutty taste of sesame. The secret of success is to use plastic wrap with your bamboo mat.

Method

1 Cover the bamboo mat with a sheet of plastic wrap and set aside.
2 Toast a sheet of nori as directed for nori rolls (see recipe left), then place it on a cutting board and spread with the prepared sushi rice, patting it out all the way to the edges of the seaweed.
3 Scatter 1 tbsp of white or black sesame seeds (or a mixture of the two) evenly over the layer of rice.
4 Carefully pick up the layered nori and turn it over onto the bamboo mat, so that the side with the sesame seeds lies on the plastic wrap.
5 Arrange you chosen fillings such as pieces of pitted umeboshi plum, or finely shredded carrot and cucumber, in a line along the centre of the seaweed.
6 Roll up into a cylinder using the method shown for norimaki above, then cut each cylinder of sushi into 3 cm pieces and serve.

hand-shaping nigiri sushi

This type of hand-moulded sushi looks relatively easy to make, however the Japanese consider it one of the most difficult types to get exactly right and usually leave it to the skills of the professional sushi chef. It takes trained hands to shape the rice gently but firmly so that it is cohesive enough to pick up in one piece while still being deliciously light-textured once you have popped it in your mouth.

Method

1 Wet your hands with acidulated water to prevent the rice sticking. Take a handful of cooked vinegared rice and mould it into a neat oblong measuring about 5 cm x 2 cm x 2 cm. Using your finger, smear a little wasabi paste along the top of the rice.
2 Cover with a piece of thinly sliced raw tuna, salmon, sea bream or skinned squid, cut so that it measures about 7 cm x 3 cm. Alternatively, top the moulded rice with a cooked tiger prawn, peeled and split open along the belly so that it sits flat on the rice. You can also make nigiri sushi with rolled omelette (see page 58), cutting it into pieces measuring 7 cm x 3 cm x 1 cm, and omitting the wasabi paste.

sushi

Japanese sushi chefs train for many years to perfect their craft, yet some types of sushi are easy to make at home. The rice may be shaped into oblongs and topped with a variety of seafood (known as nigiri sushi), or wrapped with sheets of nori seaweed.

Serves 4

Preparation time: 40-60 minutes

nori rolls

Tools	Ingredients
Sharp knife	a few pieces of deseeded
Chopping board	cucumber, pickled
Bamboo mat	radish (daikon), or
Wooden spatula	fresh tuna fillet
	2 sheets nori seaweed
	vinegared sushi rice
	(see recipe right)
	½–1 tsp wasabi paste
	pickled ginger and soy
	sauce, to serve

Method

1 Cut the deseeded cucumber, pickled daikon or fresh tuna into batons measuring about 1 cm square and set aside.

2 Take a sheet of dry nori seaweed and gently warm it over a gas flame, holding it about 7–8 cm from the flame.

3 Place the bamboo mat on a dry chopping board and lay the toasted nori on top. Add 2-3 tbsp of the cooked vinegared rice and gently spread it out over the nori until the layer of rice is thin and measures about 12 cm x 8 cm. Leave a gap of 1.5 cm between the edge of the rice and that of the nori.

4 Use your finger to smear a faint line of wasabi along the centre of the rice, then cover it with a strip of your chosen filling.

5 Pick up the mat at the near side and roll it over to meet the other side, enclosing the rice and filling in the nori (see page opposite). Roll the cylinder in the mat a little to help it firm up.

6 Remove the cylinder from the bamboo mat and set aside to rest, seam-side down, while you repeat the rolling process with the remaining ingredients.

7 Using a sharp knife, cut each cylinder into 3 cm pieces. Arrange the sushi on a sushi bench or other serving plate and serve with pickled ginger, soy sauce and a dab of extra wasabi paste if desired.

sushi rice

Tools	Ingredients
Colander	300 g Japanese sushi rice
Electric rice cooker	50 ml rice vinegar
Wooden cooling tub	1 tbsp sugar
Fan	1 tsp salt
Small saucepan	
Wooden spatula	

Method

1 Wash the rice and leave to drain for 30 minutes. Place it in the rice cooker with enough cold water to rise 3 cm above the level of the rice, then switch on the cooker. When done, transfer the cooked rice to the cooling tub.

2 Mix the vinegar, sugar and salt in a small pan and place over a medium heat until the sugar has dissolved. Cool using the fan.

3 Add the vinegar to the rice and mix gently for 2 minutes.

rice cookers, pots and pans

The Japanese are extremely fond of simmered dishes that are not unlike the casseroles of Europe. Indeed, a full and well-balanced Japanese meal would always contain a simmered dish, along with something grilled, something steamed, a few deep-fried morsels, a sautéed dish and a plate of vinegar-marinated foods or dressed salad. These pots and pans help to produce a real feast.

1 Omelette Pan Known as a makiyaki-nabe, the Japanese omelette pan is oblong or square with a wooden handle, and essential for the preparation of rolled egg dishes (dashimaki) for which the Japanese are renowned. Omelette pans can be made of heavy copper with tin coating (which is the most expensive), cast iron, or heavyweight aluminium with a nonstick surface. They should be used for nothing else but eggs, and seasoned with a little oil before each use.

2 Earthenware casserole Warming simmered dishes are traditional to Japanese cuisine and the favoured utensil is an earthenware casserole called a do nabe. It is often intricately patterned as it is taken directly from the oven to the table.

3 Japanese rice cooker Although this utensil is used throughout Asia, it is a Japanese invention, first produced around 80 years ago. Over the decades,

the basic pot has been modernised and altered to serve the purpose better, with all sorts of innovations including thermostatic control and warming capability. The rice cooker consists of an inner aluminium pot within an outer one that has a spring base at the bottom. Heat is generated around the sides between the two pots. The machine works on the principle of weight; when all the water has been absorbed, the inner pot, now lighter, springs up and the electric power is cut off automatically. No more burnt or scorched rice! Electric rice cookers can be used for making soups, but in this case have to be switched off manually. They can even be used for Korean firepots and fondues. Sizes range from small models for two people, to huge catering machines that can prepare rice for up to 50 people.

4 Tempura pot Some people think the Chinese wok can be used for tempura, but this is not true. A Japanese tempura pot has straighter sides, and is designed to keep the oil at an even temperature, which is imperative for perfect tempura. A wok, on the other hand, maintains different temperatures at different points and is too erratic for delicate deep-frying. Tempura pots come with their own racks so that the fried food can be placed on the side to drain.

5 Drop lid Known as an otoshibuta in Japan, this wooden lid, normally made of cedar, is placed inside saucepans during cooking. This helps to concentrate the heat on the food being cooked, and to stop the food bouncing around and breaking up during boiling.

tempura prawns

Japanese chefs make deep-frying an art form. Only the best oil is used, and the resulting foods are remarkably grease-free, crisp on the outside and perfectly cooked on the inside. The secret lies in the feather-light batter made at the very last moment before frying. This recipe can be easily adapted to cook other ingredients – virtually any vegetable can be cooked in this style.

Serves 4
Preparation time: 40 minutes

Tools	Ingredients
Knife	8 tiger prawns,
Chopping board	shelled with tails left on
Tempura pot	oil for deep-frying
Large bowl	grated daikon, soy sauce and
Fine sieve	wasabi paste, to serve
Small bowl	*For the batter*
Bamboo draining basket	3 tbsp plain flour,
Cooking chopsticks	plus extra for dusting
Grater	1 tbsp cornflour
	½ tsp baking powder
	600 ml ice-cold water
	1 large egg white

Method

1 Devein the prawns and make a deep slit down the back. Spread out each prawn like a butterfly and press down gently.

2 In the tempura pot, heat the oil to 180°C. To test the temperature, fry a cube of bread and if it turns golden brown in 1 minute, the oil is ready to cook with.

3 Meanwhile make the batter. Sift the flours and baking powder into a bowl. Add the ice-cold water a little at a time, whisking to combine.

4 In a separate bowl, beat the egg white until stiff peaks form, then fold it into the batter.

5 To cook, dip each prawn into a little plain flour and then into the batter and deep-fry for 2-3 minutes.

6 Drain on kitchen paper and serve with grated daikon, soy sauce and a little wasabi paste.

Variation: To make aubergine and okra tempura, slice 1 aubergine lengthways then into half circles about 1 cm thick. Remove the stem ends from a handful of okra. Dip the vegetables into the batter and transfer to the hot oil.

making a rolled omelette

The omelette is cooked in three stages, as a minimum of three layers is required, but you can do more if you like. Mix the eggs lightly, without beating, as you do not want a fluffy omelette.

Method

1 In a mixing bowl, dissolve the sugar in the dashi, soy sauce and mirin to make a broth. Crack the eggs into a separate bowl and lightly. Making sure the broth is at room temperature, pour in the beaten egg and lightly combine.
2 Heat the omelette pan until quite hot, then brush lightly with oil.
3 If you are using a large pan, pour one-third of the egg mixture into the pan. If using a smaller pan, pour in one-sixth of the mixture. Tilt the pan backwards and forwards as you pour until you have a very thin layer of egg just covering the base (top left). The egg should immediately sizzle around the edges. Cook over a medium heat until the egg is cooked around the edge but soft and runny on top.
4 Using chopsticks or a spatula, carefully roll up the cooked omelette (top right), and gently push it to the back of the pan.
5 Brush the empty base of the pan with oil, then push the roll away and brush underneath it too. Push the roll back, all the time keeping the pan on the heat.
6 Pour another third (or sixth) of the mixture onto the empty base (centre left), tilting the pan and lifting the cooked roll so the liquid egg flows underneath (centre right). Cook until almost done as before.
7 Using the first roll of omelette as the core, roll up the second section around it (bottom left).
8 If using a large pan, repeat the process with the final third of the mixture. If using a small pan, repeat the process with batches of the remaining mixture, rolling each new omelette around the previously cooked one. Tip the completed egg roll from the pan (bottom right) and set aside to cool.
9 Cut the omelette into 5 cm pieces and serve either alone, or if preferred, sitting on a wad of sushi rice, with a thin strip of nori wrapped around the middle.

rolled omelette

Tools	Ingredients
Mixing bowl	*For the broth*
Small bowl	1 tsp sugar
Omelette pan	4 tbsp dashi
Small pastry brush	2 tsp light soy sauce
Chopsticks or wooden	1 tbsp mirin
spatula	*For the omelette*
Knife	6 eggs
	½ tsp salt
	oil for frying
	prepared sushi rice *(optional)*
	½ sheet nori seaweed, cut into strips about 1.5 cm wide and 8 cm long *(optional)*

rolled omelette

Japan's distinctive sweetened egg roll, the tamagoyaki, is a common sight in sushi bars. The recipe here comes from *Food of Japan* author and film maker shirley booth, who lived in the country for six years and studied Zen temple cookery. 'If you become quite deft at this and really want to show off, you can put a sheet of nori between one of the layers as you cook,' she says. 'Once rolled and then cut through it will reveal an impressive spiral effect.'

Serves 4

Preparation time: 30 minutes

grilling and tabletop cooking

Given the diminutive nature of most Japanese homes, large kitchens and dining rooms are rare luxuries. However from this restriction has evolved a tradition of cooking at the table, thus minimising the use of small kitchens. Grilled foods have always been a speciality in Japan, whether enjoyed as a simple domestic sizzling affair or as the high drama in a teppanyaki restaurant.

to be cooked at the table. The one shown here is a gas-fired model that works on disposable cartridges that are inserted in the base. These machines are useful for outdoor cooking too. Also available are small tabletop burners that can gently cook delicate foods but which are more practical for keeping warm at the table dishes that have already been cooked.

3 Teppanyaki griddle The Japanese name derives from the Chinese word for 'iron pan'. This is a domestic version of the massive restaurant teppanyaki. Although modern in concept, it harks back to post-Iron Age Japan when nomadic warriors cooked on makeshift iron sheets over charcoal fires. Electric or otherwise, the teppanyaki is no more than a flat iron pan for cooking at the table dishes for which minimal oil is required.

4, 5 Sukiyaki pans Sukiyaki is a sautéed dish of chicken or beef with assorted vegetables. Most Japanese homes are small and the cooking range is often no more than a tiny

stove, so cooking at a charcoal or gas ring at the dining table is expedient. There is no need for an additional utensil to serve the cooked dish as diners help themselves straight from the pan. The traditional round cast-iron sukiyaki pot would be used over a charcoal or gas fire, however electric versions are available.

6 Korean firepot Related to the steamboat (see page 128), firepots are also known as sin sul lo and come in aluminium or brass. When using the charcoal-burning type of firepot shown here, it is wise to place it on a heavy piece of wood to prevent scorching your tabletop. Also watch out for sparks from the burning charcoal, and ensure the dining room has adequate ventilation. Electric firepots are cleaner and safer to use and have thermostat control to prevent overboiling, but they do lack the rustic appeal.

Hibachi barbecue (*not shown*) These Japanese portable barbecues are made of cast iron and fired by charcoal. They have short legs so they can be set on the ground, or on a tabletop if the table is fireproof. The height above the charcoal of the grill rack can be adjusted to suit the type of food being cooked.

1 Ridged griddle A small, portable barbecue grill, this useful item has a corrugated cooking surface so that fat from the food being grilled (typically meat, poultry or fish) easily drips away. The griddle can be placed over a gas or charcoal heat source. Electric models are also available.

2 Tabletop burner Indispensable to Korean and Japanese homes is the tabletop burner, which allows dishes

chicken yakitori

Yakitori, bite-sized pieces of chicken threaded on skewers and grilled over charcoal, is Japan's most popular street food and a favourite bar snack. According to distinguished Japanese food writer emi kazuko, who has provided this recipe, the bird's leg meat is most commonly used but other parts of the chicken, especially the liver, are also excellent cooked in this way.

Serves 4-8

Preparation time: 25 minutes, plus 30 minutes soaking

Tools	Ingredients
12-16 bamboo skewers	6-8 chicken thighs, about
Sharp knife	450 g, skinned and boned
Small saucepan	lemon wedges and
Hibachi grill	powdered sansho, to serve
Basting brush	*For the tare sauce*
	3 tbsp sake
	scant 5 tbsp shoyu
	1 tbsp mirin
	1 tbsp sugar

Method

1 Soak the bamboo skewers in water for 30 minutes.

2 Cut the chicken thighs into 2 cm square pieces and thread 4 pieces onto each skewer.

3 Combine all the ingredients for the tare sauce in a small saucepan and bring to the boil, stirring. Simmer for 5 minutes, then remove from the heat.

4 Heat the grill until hot. Cook the skewered chicken until lightly browned all over. Remove the skewers from the heat, one at a time, and baste with the tare sauce. Return to the heat to dry the sauce, then remove and baste with more sauce.

5 Repeat this process a few more times until all the chicken pieces are golden brown. Serve with lemon wedges and powdered sansho, or chilli pepper.

hibachi tuna with maui onion salad

This classy dinner party recipe comes from chef roy yamaguchi of Roy's Restaurants in the USA. 'If you have any leftover marinade, refrigerate it for another time,' he says. 'Just bring it to the boil and keep adding to it. My father had a batch that he kept going for 16 years!'

Serves 4

Preparation time: 1 hour

Tools	Ingredients
2 mixing bowls	4 tuna fillets, about 200 g each
	For the marinade
Saucepan	225 ml soy sauce
Hibachi grill	1 tbsp chopped garlic
Sharp knife	1 tbsp minced ginger
Chopping board	50 g spring onions, sliced
	95 g sugar
Wok and ladle	*For the ponzu sauce*
	500 ml sake
	500 ml mirin
	½ tsp chilli flakes
	10 cm kombu seaweed
	275 ml soy sauce
	juice of 3 lemons
	juice of 1 lime
	juice of 1 orange
	For the maui onion salad
	1 large carrot
	1 small Maui onion
	1½ Japanese cucumbers, deseeded
	110 g Japanese spice sprouts
	8 tbsp pickled ginger
	1 tbsp oil
	110 g beansprouts
	½ tbsp toasted white sesame seeds
	½ tbsp black sesame seeds
	juice of 1 lemon

Method

1 Combine the marinade ingredients in a large mixing bowl and marinate the tuna for 1 hour.

2 Meanwhile, to make the ponzu sauce, boil the sake, mirin, chilli flakes and kombu in a saucepan over a high heat for 10 minutes. Remove the pan from the heat and add the soy sauce and citrus juices. Leave the kombu in the sauce until serving time.

3 About 30 minutes or so before you are ready to serve, get a hibachi or barbecue grill ready.

4 To make the salad, shred the carrot, finely slice the onion and julienne the cucumber. Combine them with the spice sprouts and pickled ginger in a mixing bowl. Heat the oil in a wok and stir-fry the beansprouts over a high heat for 15 seconds. Transfer them to the mixing bowl and toss with the vegetables.

5 Remove the tuna from the marinade and grill over a high heat for 45-60 seconds per side.

6 Divide the salad between 4 serving plates. Sprinkle with the sesame seeds and lemon juice. Place the tuna on top and spoon the ponzu sauce over the fish.

korean firepot

When chill is in the air, try this heart-warming mode of cooking. Electric firepots are less smoky and easier to handle than those that require charcoal, however you can keep a charcoal-burning pot warm with tealights if you prefer. This dish differs slightly to the steamboats of Southeast Asia and China in that the ingredients are cooked all at once and diners then help themselves.

Serves 8-10
Preparation time: 35 minutes

Ingredients

400 g fillet beef, thinly sliced
2 large onions, thinly sliced
1.5 litres beef or other meat stock
5 eggs
4 tbsp flour
400 g white fish fillet, thinly sliced
200 ml oil
5 spring onions, sliced diagonally
2 carrots, julienned
400 g pine kernels or walnuts

Tools

Cleaver
Chopping board
Firepot
Wok and ladle
Wire mesh spoons

Method

1 If using a charcoal firepot, light the charcoal (top left) and have all the ingredients prepared (centre). Put the beef, onions and stock in the firepot and bring to the boil.

2 Meanwhile, beat 2 eggs lightly in a small bowl. Place the flour in a dish and dip the strips of fish in the egg then into the flour to coat.

3 Heat a little oil in a wok and stir-fry the fish until cooked. Add it to the firepot.

4 Beat the remaining 3 eggs in a small bowl. Cook into an omelette in the wok, then cool and slice into thin strips.

5 Add the omelette, spring onions and carrots to the firepot. Top with the pine kernels or walnuts and simmer for 10 minutes before letting guests help themselves, each dipping into the stock with their own wire mesh spoon (top right) to lift small portions of food.

small cooking tools

Japanese cuisine is known for its simplicity and minimalism, and although the typical Japanese kitchen is small – even cramped – there is a particular fondness for having the right tool for each job. Quality is valued above quantity. The Japanese have a great appreciation of natural materials such as wood and bamboo, and place strong emphasis on visual appeal, so their tools also often have a synergy between colours, shapes and textures.

1 Suribachi The sturdy Japanese grinding bowl is reminiscent of an apothecary's ceramic mortar. The high-fired pottery bowl is scored with hundreds of tiny grooves on the inside. This textured interior acts like the surface of a grater and, in tandem with the wooden pestle, processes garlic, ginger, kernels and seeds with amazing efficiency. The pestles come in various lengths, from 10 cm to 18 cm. The longer and therefore heavier the pestle is, the better the leverage will be. To use a suribachi, rotate the pestle and press down so the rounded end crushes the contents against the grooves of the bowl.

2 Square wire mesh strainer Known as a zaru, this wire mesh basket is used as a straining basket for items such as noodles. Bamboo versions are also available.

3 Three-section grater This grater-cum-server is intended for small pieces of food, especially those used as condiments, such as garlic, ginger and daikon. It is designed to be taken to the table.

4, 5 Cooking chopsticks Some 35 cm long and made of wood or bamboo, these chopsticks are indispensable in the Japanese kitchen for manipulating and turning all kinds of foods using only one hand. The length means that the cook can stay away from spluttering fat while deep-frying. Some models are held together by string, others are shaped like tongs. The tips may be flat or, more usually, pointed.

6 Mandolin This curiously named and notoriously sharp implement actually looks like the musical instrument of old and has a case made of hard plastic or metal. It comes with several detachable blades that slot into the centre for efficient slicing, grating, crinkle cutting, shredding and julienne cutting. Mandolins are especially good for making paper-thin slices of hard vegetables such as carrot and daikon, and need not be restricted to Japanese vegetables – cabbage and baby artichokes are also good sliced with this machine. Premium models offer better protection for the hand and are the safest to use.

7 Grater The larger teeth of this two-sectioned grater are used to coarsely grate daikon, while ingredients such as ginger and wasabi root are finely processed using the small teeth. These graters may be ceramic, or made from metal or plastic.

8 Metal spatula This tool is ideal for turning pieces of fish during cooking

steamed snapper with soy daikon fumet

Healthy eating East-meets-West-style is the speciality of doc cheng's restaurant in Raffles Hotel, Singapore, from where this deliciously light recipe inspired by Japanese cooking comes. The original is made with the Japanese or tai variety of snapper, however any good quality prime white fish such as sea bass will do for this dish, as long as it is beautifully fresh.
Serves 4
Preparation time: 40 minutes, plus one hour standing

Tools	Ingredients
Medium pot	4 whole small snapper or
Grater	large fillets, about 130 g each
Fine sieve	8 tbsp oil
Shredder	4 tbsp sesame oil
Cleaver	1 tbsp finely shredded ginger
Wire rack	90 g spring onion, julienned
Small pot	salt and pepper
	For the fumet
	450 ml water
	1 piece kombu seaweed
	30 g bonito flakes
	125 g daikon, shredded
	120 ml soy sauce
	4 shiso leaves, finely chopped

Method

1 To make the fumet, place the water and kombu in a pot and bring to the boil. Turn off the heat and add the bonito shavings. Set aside to stand for 1 hour.
2 Strain the fumet, discarding the solids. Add the daikon, soy sauce and shiso leaves.
3 Season the snapper with salt and pepper and place in the steamer over boiling water. Cover and steam for 4-6 minutes over a medium heat or until cooked.
4 Meanwhile, gently heat the neutral-flavoured oil and the sesame oil in a small saucepan.
5 When the fish is done, transfer to a deep serving dish. Scatter with the ginger and spring onions, then ladle the fumet over and around the fish.
6 Spoon the hot oil mixture over the ginger and spring onions and serve immediately.

roast pumpkin with cashew nut and gomaiso dressing

At The Providores restaurant in London, New Zealand-born chef peter gordon prepares his trademark fusion style of cooking for an adoring, sophisticated crowd. This recipe however is from Peter's book on home cooking. 'The most important ingredient in this relatively simple dish is the pumpkin, so make sure you hunt out the sweetest and tastiest there is,' he says.

Serves 4-8
Preparation time: 1 hour 30 minutes

Tools	Ingredients
Sharp knife	1.5 kg pumpkin, peeled and deseeded
Chopping board	2 tbsp sesame oil
Large ovenproof dish	400 ml boiling water
Suribachi	a large bunch of rocket
Mixing bowl	50 g toasted sesame seeds
	20 g sea salt flakes
	120 g cashew nuts, toasted and finely chopped
	100 ml mirin
	100 ml lemon juice
	salt and pepper

Method

1 Preheat the oven to 180°C/Gas 4. Cut the pumpkin into 8 even-sized chunks and place them in an oven-proof dish. Lightly season with salt and pepper, drizzle over the sesame oil, then pour in the boiling water. Roast in the top part of the oven until tender, 40-80 minutes depending on the type of pumpkin.

2 Meanwhile, make the dressing. Using the suribachi, grind the lightly toasted sesame seeds and sea salt together to give a fine powder. Transfer to a mixing bowl and add the chopped cashew nuts, mirin and lemon juice. Mix well and leave to stand until the pumpkin is cooked.

3 Arrange the hot pumpkin on a plate and scatter some rocket on top of it. Adjust the seasoning of the dressing to taste, then pour it over the rocket and serve.

aubergine salad with tart sesame dressing

This recipe from Tokyo-based cookery expert elizabeth andoh makes a terrific summer salad when chilled and served on crisp leaves. She says: 'The same dressing, by the way, could transform the most mundane tomato and cucumber slices into an interesting Oriental salad.'

Serves 2-3

Preparation time: 20 minutes

Tools	Ingredients
Knife	1 aubergine, about 350 g
Chopping board	1 tbsp white sesame seeds
Bowl	½ tsp sugar
Colander	1 tbsp soy sauce
Pot	1 tbsp rice vinegar
Frying pan	a pinch of salt
Suribachi	½ tbsp water or dashi
	crisp salad leaves, to serve *(optional)*

Method

1 Peel the aubergine and cut it into 0.5 cm-thick diagonal slices. Cut these slices into 0.5 cm-thick strips and soak them in a bowl of cold water for 5-6 minutes to remove any bitterness and avoid discoloration.
2 Drain the aubergine, then blanch it in a pot of boiling salted water for 2-3 minutes. Drain the cooked aubergine strips and pat them dry to remove excess moisture.
3 In a heavy-based frying pan, dry-roast the sesame seeds and crush them, while still warm, in the suribachi.
4 Add the remaining ingredients, one at a time, stirring and grinding after each new addition.
5 Just before serving, toss the aubergine strips in the tart sesame dressing. Serve the salad at room temperature, or chilled and arranged on crisp salad leaves if preferred.

serving dishes and lacquer ware

In keeping with the insistence on serving foods in tandem with the seasons, most Japanese homes have separate sets of dishes and serving utensils for each season. Each item is carefully chosen to reflect the right synergy. Lacquer has been a part of Japanese table art for centuries, and some pieces can be very fine. In Korea similar serving dishes are used, though there are a few unique items.

1 Larger bowls Soup noodle dishes, usually a meal in themselves, are a highly enjoyable part of Japanese cuisine and typically served in large bowls such as this.

2 Soup spoon These spoons are used in Japan for dishes such as soup noodles, where the bowl is too large to be lifted to the lips.

3 Chopsticks and rest Japanese chopsticks taper to a point. Even though disposable sets are commonplace, beautifully decorated chopsticks are considered a special gift and presented in stunning packages. The rest is an elegant means of ensuring the food-stained tips of the chopsticks do not touch the dining table.

4 Plate In Japanese cuisine, flat plates are used for many dishes, not specifically for fried rice or noodles as in Chinese service. They may be round, square or oblong.

5 Lacquer soup bowl Japanese soups are served in these lidded lacquer bowls rather than in porcelain or pottery ones. The lids efficiently keep the heat in and the resulting steam can make it very tight. You remove the lid by applying gentle pressure around the rim of the bowl. The soup inside is then sipped delicately from the bowl, as though it were a cup.

6 Rice bowl Whether made of lacquer or porcelain, Japanese rice bowls have a gentler curvature than the traditional round, squat Chinese rice bowls.

7 Condiment dishes Shape and texture are important at the Japanese table, however, unlike Chinese culture where sharp corners and square shapes symbolise evil and death, there is no negative symbolism associated with them in Japan. Small dishes such as these are used for serving condiments and dipping sauces.

8 Korean chopsticks and spoon Unlike the Japanese, the Koreans commonly use spoons. They also favour long pointed chopsticks made of wood or metal.

9 Soba basket Known as a zaru, this square bamboo rack is specially designed for serving cold soba noodles.

10 Woven bamboo basket This small basket can serve as a napkin holder at the dining table, or be used to present a single large sushi roll.

11 Bibimbap bowl A heavy stone bowl on a wooden bench, this is used for serving Korea's famous bibimbap.

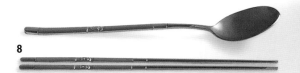

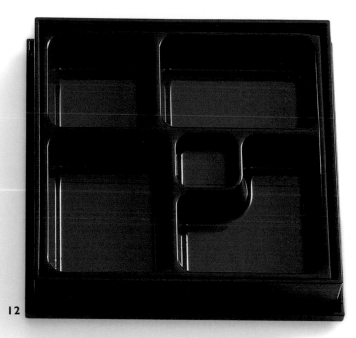

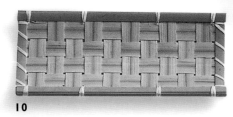

12 Bento boxes Compartmentalised lacquer boxes called bento are used to serve complete meals. With their stunning and varied designs, individual boxes and large bento sets are considered collectors' items by many people, even the disposable models produced for lunch and snack sales on trains. This style of bento box is used to serve food during intermission at plays.

13 Sushi bench Looking like a low stool of porcelain or pale wood, a sushi bench is only used to serve sushi and sashimi portions. The idea is to create a harmony of colour and texture: jewel-like colours and rich textures of raw fish against the pale, smooth bench.

14 Porcelain rice scoop Japanese rice scoops are flat and often made of porcelain with beautiful designs. Because the country's rice is starchy, a flat scoop does the job easily and without spillage.

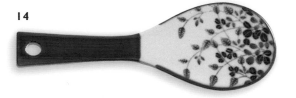

bibimbap

One of the most popular dishes in Korea, bibimbap incorporates a variety of different vegetables (and sometimes meat) mixed with peppery sauce. It is always served over plain rice and, for panache, may be presented in this traditional heavy granite bowl mounted on a wooden frame.

Serves 4
Preparation time: 30 minutes

Tools

Rice cooker
Mixing bowl
Pot
Cleaver
Chopping board
Wok and ladle
Bibimbap bowl
Colander

Ingredients

8 dried mushrooms
200 g jasmine rice
1 small carrot, julienned
2 yard-long beans, julienned
100 g beansprouts
6 large leaves bok choy, sliced
2 eggs
1 tsp black pepper
2 tbsp gochugang sauce
200 g minced beef
3 tbsp sesame oil
2 tbsp vegetable oil
100 ml water

Method

1 Soak the dried mushrooms in a bowl of warm water for about 20 minutes until soft. Meanwhile, cook the rice in the rice cooker until tender.
2 In a large pot of boiling water, cook the carrots, beans and beansprouts for 5 minutes, then drain in the colander.
3 Drain and quarter the softened mushrooms.
4 Heat 2 tbsp oil in the wok and fry the minced beef for 2 minutes. Add the pepper and gochugang sauce and stir-fry for 1 minute. Add the blanched vegetables and continue stir-frying for 2 minutes.
5 Add the bok choy and mushrooms and stir-fry for 2 minutes, then mix in the sesame oil and water. Cook for 2 minutes.
6 Place the rice in the bibimbap bowl and cover with the meat mixture.
7 Clean out the wok, fry the eggs in 1 tbsp oil. When cooked, place the eggs on the bibimbap and then serve.

simmered sweet tofu

This is one of the many simmered dishes in Japanese cuisine but often served cold as a starter, when it looks fabulous presented on a simple plate. The caramelized sugar gives the sauce a slightly bittersweet taste. You can use any type of tofu for this dish, including egg-flavoured.

Serves 1-2
Preparation time: 20 minutes

Tools	Ingredients	Method
Cleaver	1 tbsp oil	**1** Heat the oil in a pan. Add the sugar and cook until it caramelizes and turns light brown. Remove from the heat.
Chopping board	1 tbsp sugar	
Small pot	300 g tofu	**2** Add the soy sauce and water, then return the pan to the heat and bring to a gentle simmer.
Ladle	1 tbsp light soy sauce	
	1 tsp cornflour	**3** Dissolve the cornflour in a little extra water and add it to the sauce. Cook until it thickens and turns glossy.
	130 ml water	
	½ spring onion, finely shredded	**4** Cut the tofu into cubes, add to the pan and simmer for 1 minute. **5** Serve hot scattered with the spring onions, or allow to cool then chill for 1 hour to serve as a cold starter.

salt-grilled trout

It is fun to serve a meal, especially lunch, in bento boxes and this salt-grilled trout recipe is an ideal dish to feature as the main component. It can also be served as part of a Japanese meal, paired with daikon pickle. If fish does not take your fancy, chicken yakitori (see page 61) is another good recipe for bento boxes. Serve with a mound of cold cooked sticky rice sprinkled with black sesame seeds, a little green salad, plus some pickled ginger.

Serves 4
Preparation time: 25 minutes

Tools	Ingredients
Kitchen carver or fish knife	4 large trout
Chopping board	2 tbsp fine table salt
Metal or bamboo skewers	4 heaped tbsp daikon pickle (see page 50)
Hibachi barbecue	2 tbsp lemon juice
	oil for basting

Method

1 Gut and clean the trout but leave it whole. Pat the fish dry and salt it liberally both inside and out. Leave the salted fish to stand for 25 minutes at room temperature.

2 Using metal or bamboo skewers, pierce each trout through the head just behind the eye and across 5 cm of the lower body towards the tail. You should be able to lift the trout by holding the hooked end of the skewer.

3 Grill over charcoal for 6 minutes on each side, basting with a little oil during cooking to prevent dryness.

4 When the fish is done, gently remove the skewers and place on a serving plate, or cut up for inclusion in a bento box. Sprinkle a little lemon juice over the fish and serve with the daikon pickle.

chilled soba noodles

High summer in Japan can be oppressive, with unforgiving 40°C heat and high humidity. Small wonder then that chilled noodles are a great comfort, innocent of all but the lightest mirin dressing. Traditionally, this dish is served in a smart bamboo box with a separate beaker of dipping sauce that is held close to the chest while eating to minimise splashing.

Serves 4

Preparation time: 15 minutes

Tools	Ingredients
Large pot	130 g soba or thin somen noodles
Small pot	300 ml dashi stock
Wire mesh drainer	150 ml mirin
	60 ml soy sauce
	1 tbsp sesame oil

Method

1 Bring a large pot of water to a rolling boil. Add the noodles gradually so as not to stop the boiling action. Stir gently to prevent sticking and cook according to the packet instructions until just softer than al dente.
2 Meanwhile, make the dipping sauce. Combine the dashi, mirin and soy sauce in a small saucepan, bring to the boil and simmer for 5 minutes. Cool the sauce quickly by placing the pan in a sink of cold water.
3 When the noodles are done, rinse them under a cold tap and set aside to drain thoroughly.
4 To serve, drizzle the noodles with the sesame oil and a little of the cold dipping sauce and toss well. Divide the noodles amongst the serving boxes and place the remaining dipping sauce in a beaker. If desired, add a couple of ice cubes to each serving, or garnish with thin strips of nori seaweed.

three simple soups

Whether it is breakfast, lunch or dinner, a nourishing soup is served at every Japanese meal. Slightly cloudy miso soups, made with one of the many varieties of soy bean paste, are perhaps the best-known but clear soups are also popular. All are based on dashi, Japan's ubiquitous stock, made from kombu seaweed and dried bonito flakes. It is available as a convenient concentrated powder.

shrimp soup

Soften a small piece of wakame seaweed in a little cold water for 10 minutes. Trim away any hard bits, then cut the remaining wakame into 2 cm pieces. Meanwhile, shell and devein 8 medium-sized raw prawns. Bring a small pot of water to the boil and blanch the prawns for 2 minutes, then drain and set aside. Bring some more water to the boil, blanch the wakame for 1 minute then rinse and drain under a cold tap. Mix 800 ml water and 1 tbsp dashi concentrate in the pot and bring to simmering point. Add salt to taste. To serve, place 2 shrimps and a small amount of wakame in a bowl and top up with the dashi. Garnish each bowl with ½ tbsp fresh coriander leaves and serve.

miso shiru

Drain 200 g tofu and cut into 2 cm cubes. In a saucepan, blend 3 tbsp miso with 800 ml water and 2 tbsp dashi concentrate and heat until the liquid just reaches scalding point. Add the cubed tofu and 4 tbsp chopped spring onions and, when they are piping hot, serve immediately.

clam soup

Gently scrub 16 clams under running water to remove all grit. Soak in a bowl of cold water for 30 minutes, then drain in a colander. Place the clams in a pot with 800 ml water and a 10 cm piece of kombu and bring to a quick boil. Remove the kombu after 5 minutes and continue to cook the clams until they are open. Scoop the clams out with a slotted ladle and set aside. If preferred, you can cut out the clam meat and serve it without the shells. Slice 2 stalks of celery thinly and add them to the stock with 2 tsp salt, 2 tbsp finely grated lemon zest and the clams. Simmer for 3 minutes and serve immediately.

tea and sake sets

Japan's famous tea ceremonies traditionally take place in rustic teahouses, the simplicity of the setting intended to enhance the meditative ritual of the formal ceremony. Green tea is drunk on these occasions, and is the preferred beverage for everyday meals. The rice wine sake can be drunk during meals, but would properly be removed from the table once the rice was served.

1 Sake set Possibly the smallest of all liquor containers, sake bottles (called tokkuri) are veritable works of art, often featuring beautiful designs reflecting Japanese life and culture. Some sake cups are so small as to be almost thimble size, as sake is meant to be drunk in small amounts. It makes sense given its potency. Deemed a drink of the Shinto Gods, Emperors and assorted Shoguns, sake is Japan's oldest drink, a clear essence of boiled rice with yeast added to begin the alcohol-making process. It is a still beverage, served warm or cold.

2 Tea cups Authentic Japanese tea sets come with five cups, never four or six, because the number five is considered lucky in Japan's mysterious system of numerology. Much taller than the cups used in China, Japanese tea cups are always made of fine porcelain or roughcast clay and are usually straight-sided. They do not have handles because the cups are meant to be raised to the lips using both hands.

3 Tea whisk In the Japanese tea ceremony, bitter-tasting powdered green tea known as matcha is gently whipped by the tea master to a froth in hot water with this delicate bamboo whisk. To the Japanese, bamboo is symbolic of longevity and reverence. Using a metal whisk is therefore completely inappropriate to the traditional ceremony, which is a calming, spiritual experience rather than a culinary one, though food is served as well as tea.

4 Teapot Japanese teapots are relatively small. Cast-iron ones such as this are expensive and generally reserved for special guests.

ice cream desserts

A relatively modern concept, green tea ice cream probably derived from the traditional Uji gori, a kind of sorbet first made in the river town of Uji south of Kyoto and famous for its green tea. Only matcha powdered green tea is used to make it. This is a modified version produced quickly by infusing the tea in vanilla ice cream. In Japanese tempura bars green tea ice cream is coated in special batter and deep-fried to give a popular sweet treat eaten at the end of a meal. Deep-fried ice cream is often thought to be a traditional Chinese dessert too, as it is sometimes served in Western Chinese restaurants, however the claim is that it was invented by Chinese immigrants to Australia. This easy version employs filo pastry rather than tempura batter or breadcrumbs to protect the ice cream from the hot oil, and could be made with any ice cream flavour.

deep-fried ice cream Place a large plate or metal tray in the freezer to chill. When it is very cold, use an ice cream scoop to form mounds of ice cream and place them on the cold plate or tray, keeping them well separated. Place in the freezer and leave until rock-hard. When ready to proceed, take 8 sheets of filo pastry, stack them on top of each other, and cut into 15 cm squares. Heat some oil for deep-frying. Working quickly, place a portion of ice cream in the centre of each pastry square, gather up the sides and pinch to seal into a parcel, wetting the edges with a brush so that they stick together and completely enclose the ice cream. Fry in the hot oil until the pastry is golden brown. Drain thoroughly and serve immediately, with a sauce of caramel, chocolate or golden syrup, if desired.

green tea ice cream Remove 400 g vanilla ice cream from the freezer and allow to soften in a mixing bowl. Meanwhile, in a saucepan, bring 150ml full-fat milk to the boil, then turn off the heat. Stir in 1 tbsp powdered green tea and set aside to steep for 20 minutes. Blend the milky tea with the softened vanilla ice cream, beating vigorously with a wooden spoon until well combined. Place in a plastic lidded container and freeze for several hours before serving.

india,
pakistan
and sri lanka

india, pakistan and sri lanka

Cooking on the subcontinent has been influenced by Greek, Mongol and Persian invaders, spice-hungry Arab traders, and periods of British, Portuguese and French rule. The civilisation stretches back some 5000 years. When coupled with the area's sweeping geographical differences, it is not surprising that the kitchens of India, Pakistan and Sri Lanka boast such a varied collection of culinary curiosities.

Geographically, the Indian subcontinent varies widely, boasting soaring mountain ranges, a dramatic coastline, deserts and the fertile plains of three great river basins. The lay of the land, as well as historical, cultural and religious differences, have produced a fascinating mix of culinary styles.

The Moghul empire fostered a rich and refined cuisine, and imports from the Middle East of dried fruit, almonds and pistachio nuts became integral features of royal banquets. Parsees in India can trace their ancestry back to Iranian roots, and despite leaving Persia back in the 1st century AD, their cooking continues to reflect classic Persian flavours. Well-known Indian sweets such as kulfi and gulab jamuns also have their origins in central Asia. Gulab means rose, and these sweets are fried balls of curd cheese dipped in rose-scented syrup. Kulfi, India's favourite frozen dessert, takes its name from the conical mould in which it is frozen and was brought to India via Kabul with the Moghuls. Delicate rice pilaus from Lucknow, and rich Hyderabad biryanis were, as they are today, made with the finest long-grain rice, embedded with spiced meat and often touched with saffron, almonds and raisins.

Popular tandoori dishes, which are characterised by spiced yogurt marinades, get their name from the clay oven in which the meat or fish is roasted. Tandoor ovens can be found across much of Asia and are also used for baking flat breads, most notably naan. Although red food colouring may be the hallmark of tandoori curry houses in the West, there are no artificial additives in traditional tandoori recipes.

While breads are the mainstay of the North Indian diet, southern states are happier with rice. South Indian cooking makes much of locally grown coconuts, curry leaves and tart tamarind flavours, while kitchens in the North Indian state of Punjab embrace their dairy products, preferring to cook favourite dishes in ghee (clarified butter), instead of oil. Recipes from Bengal, East India, are flavoured with nutty-tasting mustard oil, and a fair share of western coastal dishes from Goa brim with a colonial Portuguese influence. Many dishes are surpris-

ingly mild, depending more on the depth of spice blends than brute chilli power. That is not to say that subtlety is the norm for cooking styles across the subcontinent. Tribal dishes from states such as

ABOVE: **1** pistachios, **2** basmati rice, **3** chapatti flour, **4** paneer, **5** cashews, **6** appam flour, **7** yogurt, **8** chickpeas, **9** green lentils. OPPOSITE: **1** corn, **2** plantain, **3** aubergine, **4** jackfruit, **5** coconut, **6** mango, **7** okra, **8** spinach, **9** curry leaves.

Andhra Pradesh, South India, are loaded with what locals call the 'guntur', or 'flaming chilli', and one bite is all it takes to bring out the fire engines. Contrary to popular impression, authentic Indian cooking does not always involve hours by the grinding stone. A simple fillet of fish wrapped in a banana leaf and baked with a minimum of spices can be enjoyed with as much relish as shellfish simmered in a carefully blended broth of rich coconut milk, pounded chillies, ginger and garlic.

Indian cooks are masters at coaxing maximum flavour from humble vegetables, using deft spicing techniques and winning combinations of contrasting ingredients. Soupy lentils and pulses are served at most meals, and transformed into delicious curries with spices. The blandness of chickpeas may be offset with sour pomegranate; split lentils treated to tangy tamarind, and kidney beans simmered with gingery masala. In coastal regions such as Bengal, Kerala and Goa, the many Hindus, who do not normally consume meat, are happy to enliven daily vegetables with tiny fried shrimps and red chillies.

Over and above geographical influences, religious beliefs play a fundamental role in the varied cooking styles of India. Hindus, for example, do not eat beef, and some communities will not touch milk or honey either. Muslims demand that 'halal' meat is used in kitchens, which means that animals must be slaughtered according to their religous edicts.

Kitchen duties are certainly not taken lightly. Many wealthy Brahmins, for example, feel duty-bound to preserve the purity of their high caste by ensuring that the home-cooking is overseen by a live-in 'maharaj' (head cook), who may enter the kitchen only after bathing and having said his daily prayers.

BELOW: **1** cinnamon sticks, **2** cloves, **3** turmeric powder, **4** saffron strands, **5** dried red chillies, **6** cardamom pods, **7** fennel seeds, **8** fenugreek seeds, **9** star anise, **10** black peppercorns, **11** coriander seeds, **12** cumin seeds.

Jains follow a faith closely related to Buddhism and will not cook with onions or garlic, in the belief that both ingredients increase body temperature and inflame lusty passions. Despite the implied austerity of the phrase 'pure vegetarian cooking', the Jain community is well-known throughout India for their tasty own-made pickles, refined milky grain dishes elegantly flavoured with saffron and cardamom, and innovative ways of cooking everyday vegetables.

There are a great many similarities between the cooking of Northwestern India and Pakistan (formerly West Pakistan, from which East Pakistan split to become Bangladesh) and in fact it can be difficult to tell them apart. Pakistan is a Muslim country, where Islam eschews the eating of pork, but the cuisine features all other meats, especially lamb, and boasts many grand dishes similar to the Moghul culinary ilk. Saffron pilau, biryanis, samosas and chapattis are as Pakistani as they are Indian, and the dishes can be chilli-hot or mild and subtle.

Much of what is perceived to be Indian cooking in the West, particularly in Britain, actually hails from Bangladesh. Although separated by a distance of 1500 km from Pakistan, it echoes with the same spicy resonance. Bangladesh was once a part of the eastern province of Bengal and the influences are palpable. The coastline that caresses the Bay of Bengal has plentiful seafood, and the cooking features many fish and shellfish dishes with spices used liberally. Ghee is not used frequently, as Bangladeshi chefs tend to prefer neutral tasting fats such as vegetable, mustard and coconut oils.

Sri Lanka is the 'pearl' that hangs at the tip of the Indian crown. A tiny island of undulating landscape formerly known as Ceylon, it marked a convenient halfway point between Asia's two most active trading empires and consequently Sri Lanka has an incredibly rich culinary heritage. The best cooking is generally based on the highland village traditions. Vegetables, fruits, home-grown meats and poultry feature prominently, and the abundant local seafood enriches every Sri Lankan table.

Much of the cuisine is stamped with the influences of Arab, Indian, Malay, Portuguese, Dutch and British traders and settlers. Many Sri Lankan dishes have marked Portuguese elements, such as the use of red wine vinegar and tomatoes, as these Europeans ruled Sri Lanka for around 150 years during the 16th century. Saffron-flavoured rice came to the island from Northwestern India. Sri Lankan rotis are also similar to the flat breads of India, and the cuisine features a mouth-watering range of seafood, beef and poultry curries. The most famous Sri Lankan dishes are undoubtedly sweet hoppers (a type of noodle), and the spiced rice dish lamprios, which is derived from Dutch lampriist

processing spices, herbs and coconut

Food processors have not yet found a place in Indian kitchens, with many cooks still pledging allegiance to the large household grinding stone, and trusty pestle and mortar. The truth is that pounding ingredients extracts maximum flavours, and food processors simply do not deliver as good a result. Practical and beautiful storage containers make mixing intricate blends of dried spices, the mainstay of most Indian cooking, a quick, simple process and a joy to perform.

1 Coconut grater With this sturdy implement, pieces of coconut still in their shells can be grated simply by cranking the handle. An L-shaped metal rod is slotted through a stainless steel mount, one end featuring a crosshead with serrated edges and the other a small rubber handle. A lever attached to the rubber suction cap at the bottom of the mount forms a vacuum that secures it to any smooth surface. In South India, where fresh coconut is used daily, some households have a very large version of this contraption which incorporates a stool for sitting.

2 Herb shredder This stainless steel gadget with a handy fold-back lid is for shredding fresh herbs and aromatics. When cranked, the handle turns a sharp-tooth spindle that efficiently cuts through the ingredients inside.

3 Stone pestle and mortar Similar to that used in Southeast Asia and Indochina, this pestle and mortar set is used for grinding fresh aromatic ingredients such as garlic, onions and chillies. It may be granite or marble and comes in various sizes.

as required in useful little cup-shaped mortars such as this popular brass model with matching pestle.

5 Square table-shaped grater Here tough aluminium is shaped into a miniature table, the top punctured with holes with sharp edges facing upwards to act as a grater. A plate or tray can be placed underneath to catch the shredded food.

7 Spice box India's most useful and ubiquitous kitchen tool has to be the round stainless steel spice box. A tightly-lidded tin filled with smaller containers, it is used for storing essential spices and holds between five and seven smaller tins. Some have an additional layer for items such as cinnamon sticks to lie flat.

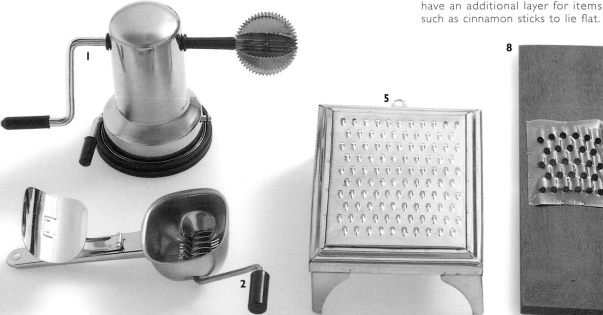

4 Brass pestle and mortar Freshness is fundamental to spice cookery and Indian cooks never keep ground spices for long as they lose their flavour and fragrance. Dried whole spices are ground in small amounts

6 Individual spice tin This single stainless steel container is useful for storing large or bulky spices such as cinnamon, bay leaves, brown cardamom pods and other dried aromatic ingredients.

8 Brass and wood coconut grater A slightly convex brass grater is mounted on a sturdy wooden frame. The protruding teeth are effective shredders of coconut, gourds and other hard ingredients.

indian spice pastes

Although spices play an integral role in every Indian meal, housewives in India insist on buying them in small quantites because they easily lose their distinctive aromas, especially when exposed to air and kept in hot, humid conditions. Spices may be used raw, but are frequently toasted or fried before further use. When toasting spices, it is preferable to toast them whole and grind them afterwards. Good Indian cooks are skilled at blending ingredients for spice pastes, and individual households take pride in handing family recipes down through the generations. The pastes are best made just prior to cooking, not in bulk, in order to maximise freshness and flavour. The following recipes demonstrate the wide range of flavours that can be achieved.

a paste for pork vindaloo
In a mortar, pound 1 small onion and 3 cloves of garlic to a paste. In a hot, dry frying pan, toast 2 tsp cumin seeds, 3 dried red chillies, ¼ star anise and a 5 cm cinnamon stick, over a low heat until they give off a nutty aroma, about 30 seconds. Remove from the pan and grind the spices to a powder before blending them with the onion and garlic. Heat 2 tbsp oil in a karahi and fry the spice mixture over a low heat, stirring continuously for 4 minutes, or until oil comes to the surface. Add 1 tsp salt, 2 tbsp malt vinegar and 5 tbsp water. Stir over a low heat until the paste (bottom left) thickens. It is now ready for the next step of cooking.

a paste for grilled chicken
This paste (top right) is for rubbing into 4 skinned chicken joints for grilling. Grind 1 tbsp grated ginger and 3 cloves garlic until fine. Add ½ tsp pounded black peppercorns and 1 tsp chilli powder. Heat 1 tbsp ghee in a karahi, and fry the paste over a low heat for 4 minutes. Add 1 tsp salt, 1 tsp sugar and 1 tbsp lemon juice. Remove from the heat, cool, then rub the spice paste over the chicken pieces.

a paste for mutton curry
To make a curry paste (top left) for 750 g cubed lamb or mutton, soak 6 dried chillies in a little warm water until soft, then pound them to a paste using the pestle and mortar. Add 1 tbsp grated ginger and grind until it is well incorporated with the chillies. In a small mixing bowl, combine 2 tbsp finely chopped onion, 1 tbsp coriander powder, 2 tsp cumin powder, 2 tsp turmeric powder and ½ tsp cinnamon powder with 1 tbsp tamarind juice to make a paste. Stir in 8 fresh curry leaves, 4 whole cardamoms, 2 tsp salt and the pounded chilli and ginger paste. To use, heat 4 tbsp oil in a karahi and gently fry the paste over a low heat for 5 minutes until the oil is released and the mixture is fragrant.

a paste for goan fish curry
To make a curry paste (bottom right) for 750 g fish, soak 5 dried chillies in a little water to soften. In a mortar, grind 1 tbsp coriander seeds and 1 tsp cumin seeds until fine. Add 1 tbsp paprika and ½ tsp turmeric powder and blend well. Remove the spices from the mortar, then grind the soaked chillies with 1 large onion, 3 cloves garlic and 1 tbsp grated ginger. Add the spice mix, 1 tsp salt and 3 tbsp water. To use, heat 4 tbsp oil in a karahi and fry the paste over a low heat for 4 minutes before adding the fish.

okra thoran

Thorans, an essential part of Keralan meals, are dishes of crunchy stir-fried vegetables flavoured with coconut and curry leaves. das sreedharan of Rasa Restaurants says his favourite school lunch was a tiffin of rice, yogurt, pickles and a crisp thoran dish such as this one. Any combination of firm vegetables can be substituted for the okra, known as bhindi in India.

Serves 4

Preparation time: 20 minutes

Tools	Ingredients
Small knife	200 g okra
Chopping board	5 tbsp oil
Karahi	1½ tbsp mustard seeds
Colander	10 curry leaves
	2 dried red chillies
	1 onion, finely chopped
	1 tsp turmeric powder
	50 g freshly grated or desiccated coconut
	salt

Method

1 Chop the okra into 1 cm pieces and set aside.

2 Heat the oil in a karahi and add the mustard seeds. As they begin to pop, add the curry leaves and chillies, then the finely chopped onion.

3 Cook, stirring, for 5 minutes until the onion softens, then stir in the turmeric powder and a little salt and stir-fry for 2 minutes. Add the chopped okra and cook for another 3-4 minutes.

4 Remove the pan from the heat and add the coconut. Mix well, then serve hot.

pots, pans and griddles

An Indian kitchen is designed to stand up to the toughest of tasks. Catering for extended families calls for cavernous karahis and enormous pots, called patilas, that are often large enough to feed a family of fourteen in one sitting. It is best to choose pans that are made from heavy-gauge

1 Karahi pan Also known as a kadai or cheena chatti, this utensil is not very different in shape from the Chinese wok, but most karahis are smaller in size. In India they usually have a rounded base, however most karahis available in the West have flat bottoms that enable them to sit straight on electric hobs. They usually have two handles and are made of cast iron, aluminium, enamel or stainless steel. The enamel karahi shown here is effectively a nonstick pot that can be scrubbed without fear of chipping the surface. Because the handles are made of the same metal as the bowl section, they can get quite hot while on the stove and therefore care must be taken when moving the pan. The karahi is used for sautéing spices, pastes and making vegetable dishes. Large models can be used for deep-frying.

2 Small karahi These small karahis, a familiar sight in restaurants, can be brought directly to the table.

3 Tawa One of the most important utensils in the Indian kitchen, these griddles are made from cast iron and often have a long handle. Tawas are used for cooking breads such as parathas and chapattis. In South India, they are used for frying dosas, pancakes made from ground rice and lentils. After 5 minutes over a medium gas flame, tawas are a good conductor of heat and cook breads evenly, without scorching. They are also ideal utensils for roasting spices.

Tawas come in many sizes; smaller ones are no larger than 10 cm in diameter, while others may be the same size as a bicycle wheel.

4 Black terracotta curry pot Traditional vessels used throughout the subcontinent for thousands of years, terracotta or clay pots often have a thick rim and are used for simmering curries and stews on charcoal-burning braziers. The model shown here is matte black metal, and in India, such equipment is often sold by weight. A lightweight pan cannot hope to hold its own against the often involved stages of frying and scraping spice pastes. Most homes in India use gas hobs, which suits the rounded bases of many patilas, tawas, and karahis. A considerable amount of heat would be lost if these tools were to be used on an electric stove. Listed below are common cooking utensils found in kitchens across the subcontinent.

with the patina of age, having been handed down through several generations of the owner's family.

5 Straight-sided aluminium pot Known as a patila in India, this is an all-purpose pot for rice and curries. Care must be taken not to cook dishes of an acidic nature in such a pan as the aluminium will react with the food. It has no handles and comes with a flat, tight-fitting lid.

6 Stainless steel pot Many cooks are fond of using stainless steel pots as they are durable and easy to clean. This round-bottomed stewing pot with copper base has a fat belly that tapers towards the lip, and is used for curries and boiling liquids.

7 Stainless steel yogurt maker Yogurt is a staple food in homes across the subcontinent and most cooks make their own on a daily basis, using a spoonful of the previous day's yogurt to set a new batch.

Stainless steel makers are more durable than their terracotta counterparts and available in many sizes.

8 Terracotta yogurt maker Terracotta crocks are thought to be the best for setting yogurt as they give a superior texture and the porous material helps to keep the yogurt cool during the hot summer.

9 Idli pan A staple breakfast dish of South India, idlis are steamed cakes made from a fermented mixture of rice and lentil flours. The batter is cooked in a steamer that resembles a large egg poacher and is made from stainless steel or aluminium. This round-bottomed steamer has two decks (some have as many as four) with moulds for four idlis on each layer. The moulds are fixed to a central rod and the idlis are cooked by the steam produced by the simmering water in the base of the pan. The rod allows easy removal.

roast chicken madurai masala

Madurai, a town in the South Indian state of Tamil Nadu, is noted for its mild dishes, of which this chicken recipe is typical. It comes from top chef CYRUS todiwala of London's Café Spice Namaste. The ingredients list may seem long, but the dish is very simple to make.

Serves 4

Preparation time: 1 hour

Tools	Ingredients
Knife	4 chicken thighs with skin
Chopping board	2 tsp salt
Lidded pot	½ tsp turmeric powder
Basting spoon	3 tbsp oil
	10 curry leaves
	½ tsp cumin seeds
	½ tsp fennel seeds
	3 bay leaves
	200 g onions, finely sliced
	1 tbsp ginger purée
	1 tbsp garlic purée
	150 g tomatoes, halved
	1 tsp coriander powder
	½ tsp chilli powder
	1 tbsp chopped fresh coriander
	10 mint leaves, shredded

Method

1 Clean the chicken thighs, removing any excess fat. Rub with salt and turmeric powder and set aside.

2 Heat the oil in a pot and add the curry leaves, cumin and fennel seeds and fry until brown, shaking the pan vigorously to prevent burning.

3 Add the bay leaves and onions and sauté until the onions are light brown. Add the ginger and garlic purées and cook, stirring, for 1 minute. Then add the tomatoes and continue to cook until almost dry.

4 Mix the coriander and chilli powders with a little water to make a paste and add it to the pan. Cook, stirring, for 1 minute, then push the fried paste aside.

5 Lay the chicken thighs in the pan skin-side down and spread the paste all over them, rubbing it in well.

6 Cover, reduce the heat and allow the chicken pieces to brown on the skin side. Add 2 tbsp of water to create steam and facilitate the cooking.

7 Turn the chicken thighs over and continue cooking for 15 minutes or until done. To test if cooked, pierce the thickest part of one thigh with a metal skewer; if the liquid that runs out is clear, the chicken is ready.

8 Add the fresh coriander and mint leaves, cover the pan and remove from the heat ready for serving.

fruit-flavoured lassi

More than just a drink, Indian lassi is a real coolant, a yogurt beverage similar to a milkshake, and the best way to quell the fire of a hot spicy curry. Plain versions come salted or sweet, with a hint of cardamom, but fruit-flavoured lassis are increasingly popular. If you prefer not to make your own yogurt, choose a mild live yogurt such as bio-yogurt, which is good for the digestive system. Most Indian stores sell ready-puréed mango, and whole jackfruit and lychees canned in their own juice are usually available in Asian shops.

To make enough mango, jackfruit or lychee lassi for 4 people, purchase at least 650 g of canned fruit in its own juice. Set aside a few small pieces of fruit to use as a garnish, then purée the remaining fruit with the juice from the can. In a large mixing bowl, beat 500 g plain yogurt until creamy, then blend in the fruit purée. Chill thoroughly. To serve, pour into tall glasses, add a little crushed ice and garnish with the reserved fruit. For a tangy variation common in Southern India, use buttermilk in place of yogurt.

spiced lamb with almonds

Not all Indian dishes call for hours by the grinding stone, yet even the simplest recipes can offer dramatic flavours, says Indian television chef roopa gulati. Simple dry dishes like this one have their origins in the desert, where water and fresh vegetables are hard to find.

Serves 4
Preparation time: 1 hour

Tools
Knife
Chopping board
Lidded pot
Small karahi
Spoon

Ingredients
500 g boned leg lamb,
   cut into 2 cm cubes
200 g yogurt
3 onions, finely sliced
4 garlic cloves, finely sliced
2 cm ginger, finely sliced
2 cm stick cinnamon
2 small bay leaves
3 cloves
¼ tsp black peppercorns
1 tsp cumin seeds
6 tbsp oil
1 blade mace
2 dried red chillies, split
   and deseeded
4 tbsp flaked almonds
2 tbsp fresh coriander leaves
a few drops of pandan leaf
   essence (optional)

Method

1 In a pot, combine the lamb, yogurt, 2 of the sliced onions, the garlic, ginger, cinnamon, bay leaves, cloves, peppercorns, cumin seeds and 4 tbsp of oil. Mix well, add a little salt and bring to a simmer. Cover tightly, reduce the heat and cook gently for about 40 minutes or until the meat is tender.

2 Once the meat is cooked, heat the remaining 2 tbsp oil in a small karahi and add the rest of the sliced onion, plus the mace and red chillies. Reduce the heat and gently fry the onions until they are very soft in texture and a nutty golden colour.

3 Stir the onion mixture and flaked almonds into the meat. Season to taste with salt and reheat the lamb as necessary. Sprinkle with the coriander leaves and a little pandan leaf essence just before serving.

naan bread

An authentic naan needs to be cooked in an authentic tandoor. The technique involves rolling out the dough, opening the lid of the tandoor and literally sticking the bread to the wall of the oven. Nevertheless, this recipe from menernosh mody of London's Franco-Indian restaurant La Porte des Indes should give good results with a domestic oven.

Serves 14

Preparation time: 40 minutes, plus 2 hours rising

Tools

Sifter
Large bowl
Rolling pin
Tawa
Baking sheets

Ingredients

900 g plain flour
1 tbsp baking powder
1 tsp sugar
1 egg, lightly beaten
300 ml milk, boiled and cooled to lukewarm
300 ml water, lukewarm
4 tbsp oil
2 tbsp sesame seeds
melted butter, for brushing
salt

Method

1 Sift the flour into a large bowl with the baking powder, sugar and some salt. Make a well in the centre and gradually add the egg, milk and water. Stir to blend the ingredients into a dough.

2 On a floured surface, knead the dough until firm. Return the dough to the bowl, cover with a warm, damp cloth and leave to rise for 30 minutes.

3 Knead the oil into the risen dough, then leave to rise again, covered with a warm, damp cloth for 1 hour or until the dough has doubled in size.

4 Punch the dough down. Divide into 14 equal-sized balls and place them on a floured tray. Cover once again with a warm, damp cloth, and set the tray of balls aside to rise for 30 minutes.

5 Heat the oven to 240°C/Gas 9 and place 2 baking sheets in it to get hot. On a lightly floured surface, roll out each ball to give a teardrop shape 0.5 cm thick and sprinkle with sesame seeds.

6 Grease the hot baking sheets and, working in batches, place the naans on them and bake for 5-6 minutes, or until golden brown and puffed. Brush with melted butter before serving.

moulds and presses

India is a nation of munchers, where crunchy snacks are distiguished by their varied shapes and textures. Many tools for snack making have remained unchanged for thousands of years, and people are often surprised that the complex spirals of spicy bites such as murukku have been created by a simple looking press. Kulfi moulds were originally made of clay, and in many old quarters of the subcontinent, these traditional ices continue to be frozen in the same pots today.

3 Kulfi moulds These cone-shaped moulds with screw-top lids are used for making kulfi, India's famous frozen dessert. Aluminium is a popular material for moulds because it cools more quickly than plastic when placed in ice. Traditionally kulfis were set in clay pots and sealed with dough.

1 Seviya press This little brass cylinder with crank handle incorporates a selection of perforated plates, each with small holes or gashes, chosen according to the shape of snacks required. The press is used for making Sri Lankan string hoppers, South Indian murukkus and other sweet and savoury snacks. Dough is pressed into the cylinder, then the top lid of the press is wound down into place. When the handle is turned, it pushes the dough out in the desired shape, ready for steaming or deep-frying.

4 Vadai maker Vadais are round, savoury rice flour cakes that look like exotic doughnuts; they originate from South India, but are popular throughout the country. The plunger on this stainless steel gadget forces the vadai dough out in a ring that is ready for frying.

2 Stainless steel ricer In the West this tool is most commonly used for mashing cooked potatoes. In South India and Sri Lanka, ricers may be employed to help shape string hoppers. Made of stainless steel, the ricer has a hinged lid that presses the dough through the perforated base when force is applied. This is done over oiled plates, or banana leaves, so that the piles of string hoppers created are ready for steaming.

string hoppers

Indian appams (idiappam in South India), Sri Lankan appe and string hoppers are from the same family. Basic recipes vary with regional differences, but rice flour and coconut milk are the main ingredients. A batter is forced through a metal mould into a tangle of thin threads, which is steamed before serving. Most Indian and Sri Lankan stores sell appam flour ready mixed for cooking.

Serves 4

Preparation time: 35 minutes

Tools	Ingredients
Mixing bowl	300 g appam flour
Ladle	150 ml coconut milk
Steamer	½ tsp salt
Seviya mould	fine brown sugar or demerara sugar,
Plate	for sprinkling
	oil for greasing

Method

1 Sieve the appam flour into a bowl and pour in the coconut milk and salt. Beat into a smooth batter with a creamy consistency.

2 Meanwhile, bring some water to a boil in a steamer and place a lightly oiled plate in the pan. Cover tightly, and allow the steam to build up.

3 To make the string hoppers, use a seviya mould fitted with a perforated disc that has notches the diameter of matchsticks cut out from it. Pour the appam batter into the mould.

4 Rotate the handle of the seviya mould over the plate in the steamer, making small mounds of appam threads. Repeat until there are enough piles to fill the plate, making sure that the sides do not touch.

5 Cover and steam for 10-15 minutes until the hoppers are fluffy and fragrant. Transfer to a serving plate and sprinkle with the sugar before serving hot.

saffron and cardamom kulfi

A favourite Indian dessert, kulfi is an ice cream traditionally made by reducing the milk over a gentle heat for a very long time. However, it is also easy to make with evaporated milk. This recipe comes from camellia panjabi who is one of India's most respected restaurateurs and cookery writers, as well as a director of England's prestigious Chutney Mary Group.

Serves 4

Preparation time: 45 minutes, plus freezing time

Tools	Ingredients
Kulfi moulds	4 tbsp sugar
Small pot	3 cardamoms pods
Wooden spoon	2 x 410 g cans evaporated milk
Cleaver	12 saffron strands
	3 tbsp double cream
	2 leaves silver leaf, to decorate, (optional)

Method

1 Add the sugar and cardamoms pods to the milk in a heavy-based saucepan and cook over a low heat for 10 minutes, stirring and scraping the sides and bottom of the pan continuously.

2 Remove the pan from the heat and discard the cardamom pods before adding the saffron. Mix well and leave to cool before stirring in the cream.

3 Fill the kulfi moulds, cover and freeze for 4–5 hours.

4 To remove the kulfis from the moulds, dip each one into hot water and press out the kulfi. Decorate with silver leaf, if desired, for festive occasions.

small cooking tools

Implements used in an Indian kitchen are rarely chosen for their good looks; cooks are far more concerned with durability, and place little emphasis on decorative embellishments. Because many of the tools pictured below are hand-crafted, quality and appearance does vary with each piece. Street markets are the best places to buy such equipment at affordable prices.

1 Long-handled scoop This long wooden scoop is ideal for stirring gravies and serving soupy lentils into small dishes. As in Southeast Asia, empty coconut shell halves are used in South India as ladles, and like this model have a stick attached that acts as the handle.

2, 3 Large wooden mashers Cooked vegetables such as spinach, aubergine and potatoes are often mashed with these fearsome-looking wooden tools. The club-shaped heads are usually grooved along the sides, which also makes them invaluable churners for yogurt-based drinks such as lassi, and home-made butter.

4, 5 Wooden spatulas This flat wooden tool is a versatile addition to the kitchen, and may be used in the same manner as wooden spoons.

6 Steel spatula A very thin flat spatula, this tool is good for turning fried eggs and flipping delicate dosas.

7 Steel basting spoon Some Indian chefs favour these comparatively flat spoons for cooking curries.

8 Tongs Because many cooking pots such as patilas do not have handles, tongs are often used to remove them from the stove. They are also an invaluable tool for turning chapattis as they cook on a griddle.

9 Round, winnowing basket of woven palm leaves In rural India, rice and other grains are winnowed after harvesting to separate the chaff from the grain. Small amounts are placed in the basket (or a flat tray of similar materials), and gently tossed in the air.

10 Tandoori skewer Tandoori meats are marinated and skewered on this long metal spear before roasting in special tandoori ovens. Such skewers require deft handling and turning, hence their length and weight.

11 Sieves This set of four different-sized mesh grids is used for sifting flours and other powders. In India, chapatti flour is always sieved before use.

tiffins and serving items

Bombay is famous for its tiffins. After vegetables and curries have been cooked, lunches are carried in tightly lidded stacked tins to offices across the city. When it comes to tableware, stainless steel is preferred to china or aluminium. Although relatively expensive, steel has a lengthy lifespan, and does not react to the acid in tangy Indian pickles.

1 Tiffin carriers The term tiffin was coined by the British while they were in India and was used to denote a light midday meal that may have included shepherd's pie and trifle for dessert. Today, tiffin boxes are a stacked tower of stainless steel containers filled with home-made chapattis or rice, lentils, vegetable curry, and perhaps a meat dish. Tiffin deliveries in Bombay have grown into a lucrative business. After lunches have been made at home, meals are collected by tiffin boys who then deliver thousands of hot meals to offices in the city. So successful is the industry that the delivery boys have formed their own trade union.

2, 3 Lunch boxes Many school children take these small boxes to school, as they are just the right size to hold a mid-morning snack. They often have built-in trays for holding pickles and relishes. Although plastic boxes are gaining popularity, these steel boxes continue to be chosen in India for their durability.

4 Thali and katori sets At Indian meals, different dishes are served together on a thali (steel plate), in separate bowls (katoris). Katoris come in many sizes and are ideal for serving individual portions of lentils, curries, sweets and yogurt. Ceremonial thalis may be ornately designed and made from copper or silver, but everyday versions are usually stainless steel or aluminium.

5 Pickle server These stainless steel sets with tiny accompanying spoons are a familiar sight in curry houses, where they are used for serving pickles and sauces. In India, dry spices such as toasted cumin and pounded chillies may be served in them too, for sprinkling over dishes.

6, 7 Rice scoops Common in all Indian homes, these metal scoops are used for serving rice at table.

palak paneer

Most homes in India make their own paneer by adding enough vinegar to boiling milk to separate the curds from the whey. The curds are then pressed for about 30 minutes, or longer if a firmer texture is preferred, to give a nutritious form of protein that is important to India's many vegetarians. In the West, ready-made paneer is now available in many supermarkets. This recipe comes from yogesh arora of the famous Tiffin Room at Raffles Hotel in Singapore.

Serves 4
Preparation time: 10 minutes

Tools	Ingredients	Method
Knife	2 tbsp oil	1 Heat the oil in a saucepan and sauté the onion and garlic until golden brown. Add the chopped ginger and green chilli and cook for a further 2 minutes.
Chopping board	1 small onion, chopped	
Karahi	1 tsp chopped garlic	
Spatula	1 tsp chopped ginger	2 Add the spinach, then the butter, cream, pepper, cardamon powder, garam masala and some salt.
	1 large green chilli, chopped	
	600 g spinach leaves, chopped	3 Mix in the paneer and stir over a moderate heat for about 2 minutes until the cheese is heated through. Adjust the seasoning to taste and serve immediately.
	2 tbsp butter	
	2 tbsp single cream	
	¼ tsp ground white pepper	
	a pinch of cardamon powder	
	a pinch of garam masala	
	200 g paneer cheese, cubed	
	salt	

lamb samosas

Perhaps the best ambassador for Pakistani and Indian cuisine abroad, samosas are versatile street snacks that may contain a variety of meat and vegetarian fillings and lend themselves to experimentation. Asian grocery stores sell ready-made samosa wrappers, though if necessary you will find filo pastry is an acceptable substitute. Tiny samosas make great cocktail snacks.

Serves 8
Preparation time: 45 minutes

Tools

Small knife
Chopping board
Small pot
Colander
Karahi
Plate
Spoon
Wire mesh ladle

Ingredients

400 g samosa wrappers
oil for deep-frying
For the filling
150 g potatoes
150 g mutton curry paste
  (see page 82)
400 g lamb mince

Method

1 To make the meat filling, peel the potatoes and cut into 1 cm cubes. Bring a pan of water to the boil and cook the potatoes for 10 minutes. Drain well and set aside in a bowl to cool.

2 Heat the curry paste in the karahi and stir in the lamb mince. Cook for 10-20 minutes over a low heat, then add the cooked potatoes. Stir for another 2 minutes and transfer to a plate to cool.

3 To shape the samosas, place about 1 tbsp of meat mixture in the middle at the end of a pastry strip (above left). Dampen the edges with a little water to help them to seal. Fold a corner of the pastry over the mixture to form a triangle (above centre), then continue folding in alternate directions to give a triangular parcel (above right).

4 Heat some oil for deep-frying in the karahi and deep-fry the samosas until golden brown. Remove with a wire mesh ladle or slotted spoon and place on kitchen paper to drain. Serve hot.

indochina

including thailand, vietnam, laos, myanmar and kampuchea

indochina
including thailand, vietnam, laos, myanmar and kampuchea

The Buddhist culture of Indochina has Hindu roots and dates back over some 3000 years to the days when India began trading with China after the Silk and Spice Routes opened. With the inevitable inter-marriages of Indian, Chinese and local peoples, the resulting culinary mix has become an endearing blend of hot, sweet, sour, aromatic and savoury flavours – often all in one dish.

For Thai cooking in particular, the keynote is the artful blend of fresh herbs and other aromatics, which are often ground to a paste and cooked in a little oil before being combined with coconut milk, tamarind juice or stock. In addition to the world-renowned green and red curries, which have evolved from early Indian influences into uniquely light concoctions, typical dishes of Thailand include satay, fish and prawn cakes, tantalising soups and salads zesty with lime and lemongrass. When it comes to presentation, the Thais are masters at transforming fruits and vegetables into glorious works of sculptured, edible art.

Kampuchean or Khmer cuisine echoes Chinese and Thai elements and, like Laotian cooking, tends to ride stickily on glutinous rice. The Mekong River that runs through the region yields abundant fish and shellfish, and these, along with vegetables, are the key ingredients, but will be augmented by free-range chickens, duck, pigeons and tiny paddy field birds. Pork and beef are rarely used, and lamb figures rarely outside the cities, where the imported meat has a ready market in tourists. At every Kampuchean meal there is a pungent dip of chillies and fish sauce. Noodle dishes are the staple fare of the rural folk but will be enriched with fish, chicken, venison and spices. Wild mushrooms and jungle greens turn up in salads, while coconut milk is the basis of simple desserts that usually employ bananas, mangoes and other tropical fruits.

The cornerstone of Myanmar meals is perfectly fluffy rice, around which is served many pickles and dips. A typical family meal will consist of rice, a hot and sour soup, fish and chicken curries, cellophane noodles, salads of leaves and indigenous greens, and always a dip of balauchaung, made of shrimp paste, chillies, lime juice and dried shrimps. Many dishes require little cooking; raw salads and pickles predominate.

The cuisine of Vietnam, a country which was once a French enclave, is a curious amalgam of Chinese, Thai and French cooking, with rice and rice noodles as the foundation, though French baguettes are often served with stir-fried dishes! Vietnamese fish sauce, called nuoc mam, is more pungent than the Thai version. The country's famous beef soups are richly aromatic with Chinese five-spice blends, but it is the noodles that truly mark Vietnamese cuisine. They feature in pho, the definitive beef noodle dish, which includes a broth that is rich with

ABOVE: **1** rice paper wrappers, **2** black rice, **3** coconut milk, **4** fish sauce, **5** shrimp paste, **6** peanuts, **7** dried shrimp, **8** rice noodles, **9** palm sugar. OPPOSITE: **1** galangal, **2** Thai mango, **3** lemongrass, **4** fresh coriander, **5** holy basil, **6** red chillies, **7** coconut, **8** limes, **9** Thai aubergines, **10** kaffir lime leaves, **11** bird's eye chillies.

cinnamon, coriander, pepper and other fine spices. Like the Thai, the Vietnamese are extremely fond of salads, but these are certainly not boring plates of lettuce leaves. Cabbage, carrots, celery, fruits and steamed chicken, for example, will be tossed in aromatic dressings of sesame oil, lime juice and sugar and strewn lavishly with peanuts, mint, fresh coriander and chillies to give wonderfully healthy dishes of vibrant, pungent flavours.

natural leaves and containers

In many parts of Asia, ingenious use is made of the local plant life as wrappers, skewers, plates, containers and other natural utensils, and these 'tools' are fundamental to the rustic flavour of the cuisines. A wonderfully sustainable resource, they play the dual role of being functional while

1 Banana leaves As large as umbrellas, subtly perfumed and extremely pliable, banana leaves are excellent for wrapping large items of food, usually whole fish for steaming, braising and grilling. They are thick enough to use as disposable plates, and are used widely as such in India and Southeast Asia as well as Indochina. Specialist stores sell them trimmed and folded and they need only a quick dip in hot water before use. Store away from cold air or else they will turn yellow and brittle within a few days.

2 Pineapple halves Thai chefs are particularly adept at playing with this succulent tropical fruit, using the flesh as an ingredient and the shell as a highly fragrant serving dish. The remaining half of the shell is used as a lid to keep the food warm during the meal. The natural juices still in the fruit enhance the dish in a magical way.

3 Lemongrass These grass-like plants have a heady and pervasive scent, especially at the root end. They are generally about 1 cm thick but when really lush, can grow to twice this girth. The thin 15 cm long leaves are usually discarded. Whole stems make natural lemon-scented skewers around which minced meat and seafood can be wrapped. When bruised and shredded at the root end, lemongrass becomes a basting brush with natural citric flavour. The plant's thick roots can be split and stuffed with minced food before grilling. The bottom 4 cm or so of the root end is typically ground with other spices and herbs to make curry pastes.

4 Pumpkin shells In Thailand, small pumpkins of about 1 kg in weight are hollowed out and filled with a mixture of egg, coconut milk and sugar, then baked until golden brown. The pumpkin meat is rendered soft and sweet, an ideal companion to the custard-like coconut and egg mixture. Larger pumpkins can be sliced into wedges and filled in the same way. Indonesians use pumpkins as receptacles for fruity curries.

5 Pandan leaves Measuring some 35 cm in length, these dark green aromatic leaves (sometimes called screwpine or kewra) have a distinctive vanilla scent.

imparting subtle fragrances to the food prepared. With so many Western countries now home to burgeoning Asian communities, the demand for these hitherto rare items is being fulfilled by air carriage, however they have been used since long before metal made its first glimmer.

When blanched and trimmed into even strips, they can be folded and shaped into little cups for coconut and rice flour puddings. Pieces are often wrapped around spiced chicken and prawns for deep-frying. Odds and ends are put to aromatic use, placed on the surface of rice and curries to give a subtle aroma. They keep for about two weeks in the vegetable drawer of the fridge. In India, pandan leaves are used to make a fragrant water that is added to dishes at the end of cooking to impart a heady aroma.

6 Bamboo leaves Often sold dried, bamboo leaves measure about 25 cm long and are around 7 cm broad at the centre, tapering to points at both ends. Traditionally used as wrappers for triangular rice dumplings in commemoration of a Chinese poet, they impart a husky aroma not unlike dried corn husks. Dried versions keep well for months and need to be soaked in hot water before use to make them pliable.

lemongrass prawn satay

Lemongrass is used as a herb throughout Southeast Asia, but here it is ingeniously employed as a skewer. You don't actually eat the lemongrass stalk as it is too fibrous, but the citrus tang it imparts to the barbecued minced prawn paste is delicious.

Serves 4

Preparation time: 40 minutes

Tools	Ingredients	Method
Cleaver	450 g fresh raw prawns, shelled and deveined	**1** Mince the prawns with the cleaver and set aside.
Pestle and mortar	3 spring onions	**2** Using the pestle and mortar, grind the spring onions, chillies and garlic until very fine. Add the minced prawns and continue to grind until the mixture resembles pâté.
Mixing bowl	3 fresh red chillies	
Large spoon	2 cloves garlic	
	2 eggs	**3** Transfer the mince to a mixing bowl and add the eggs, lime juice, fish sauce, cornflour, pepper and sugar. Mix well, kneading until the mixture is thick and dough-like in consistency.
	juice of 2 limes	
	2 tbsp fish sauce	
	1 tbsp cornflour	
	1 tsp black pepper	**4** Take about 2 tbsp of the mixture and shape it around a lemongrass stalk. Repeat with the remaining mixture and lemongrass stalks until all are used. Brush lightly with vegetable oil.
	1 tsp sugar	
	10-12 lemongrass stalks, about 12 cm long	
	2 tbsp oil	**5** Heat a charcoal brazier or grill and cook the satays for 5-8 minutes, turning frequently until the prawn mixture is slightly charred. Serve warm.

fish steamed in banana leaf

Before cooking, this Myanmar dish may be appear to be simply a spicy fish paste mixture, but the result is more than the sum of its parts – an intoxicating blend of fish meat, spices and fragrant herbs. During steaming, the mixture inside the leaves sets to become firm and sliceable.

Serves 6
Preparation time: 25 minutes

Tools

Cleaver
Chopping board
Pestle and mortar
Banana leaves
Large spoon
Small bamboo skewers
Bamboo steamer

Ingredients

3 lime leaves, very finely sliced
a small bunch of basil leaves, sliced
2 tsp salt
1 tsp sugar
750 g fish fillets
3 eggs, lightly beaten
2 tbsp oil
1 tbsp cornflour
200 ml thick coconut milk
For the spice paste
300 g onions
8 candlenuts
12 dried chillies, soaked until soft
2 tbsp coriander powder
1 tbsp shrimp paste
3 slices galangal
2 stalks lemongrass

Method

1 Grind all the ingredients for the spice paste in a mortar until fine, then mix with the lime leaves, basil leaves, salt and sugar.
2 Grind the fish coarsely and mix with beaten egg, oil, cornflour and spice paste. Knead briefly and add coconut milk until you get a buttery consistency.
3 Scald the banana leaves in boiling water and drain. Cut into pieces measuring 28 cm x 22 cm. Place 2 tbsp of fish on a piece of banana leaf.
4 Fold up the sides so that the fish paste is cradled in the leaf. With the thumb and forefinger, press one end to form two cornered edges, about 10 cm from the end (bottom left).
5 Do the same on the other side, making a parcel, with folded edges over-lapping and flush with the top edge of the long side. Secure with a bamboo skewer (bottom right). Repeat with the remaining ingredients.
6 Place the parcels in a bamboo steamer and cook for 15 minutes. Remove from the steamer, open the parcels and cut the paste – which will have set firm – into bite-size slices or cubes before serving.

pineapple fried rice

The Blue Elephant restaurants, tropical hothouses of orchids and other heady blooms, are known as much for their evocative ambience as for the quintessential Thai menu. Use the largest pineapple you can find for this recipe based on the Royal fried rice by chef chang, whose grandmother was a lady-in-waiting at the Thai Royal Court. His original dish uses a rather complex sauce which can be substituted, as it has been here, with a stock cube.

Serves 2
Preparation time: 35 minutes

Tools	Ingredients
Rice cooker	200 g Thai fragrant rice
Cleaver	4 tbsp oil
Small all-purpose knife	2 large eggs
Chopping board	60 g mixed bell peppers,
I fresh pineapple	finely diced
Spoon	2 tbsp finely diced Spanish onion
Wok and ladle	2 tbsp finely diced carrot
	60 g cooked prawns
	60 g crabmeat
	I tsp salt
	½ tsp ground white pepper
	½ tsp sugar
	I fish or vegetable stock cube,
	dissolved in 2 tbsp water
	2 spring onions, finely sliced
	2 tbsp finely chopped cucumber
	2 tbsp chopped tomato

Method

1 Cook the rice in the rice cooker. Drain and allow to cool overnight in the refrigerator.

2 Cut the pineapple in half lengthways with a cleaver. With a small knife, cut deep into the sides of each half, about I cm in from the skin. Cut all around the fruit, and right down the middle core, keeping I cm away from the skin. Make small cuts across and lift out chunks of pineapple flesh. With a spoon, scoop out the remaining bits, leaving a smooth, oval-shaped container.

3 Rake the cold cooked rice to loosen the grains. Heat the oil in the wok until very hot. Break in the eggs and cook until scrambled. Add the rice and stir-fry for 2 minutes.

4 Add the peppers, onion, carrot, prawns and crab and continue stir-frying for I minute. Add the seasonings, sugar and stock and mix well. Toss in the spring onions, stir briefly, and then remove the wok from the heat.

5 Carefully spoon the fried rice mixture to the pineapple shells and scatter with the cucumber and tomato. Garnish with some fresh coriander leaves if desired before serving.

bamboo leaf dumplings

Originating in China, these dumplings have become staple snack fare throughout Indochina, each region and food vendor having their own spicy filling. Dried bamboo leaves are sold in all Asian food stores and have to be blanched in boiling water before use to make them pliable.

Serves 4

Preparation time: 2 hours, plus overnight soaking for rice

Tools	Ingredients
Cleaver	400 g lean pork
Chopping board	3 tbsp finely chopped onion
Small pot	2 tbsp finely chopped garlic
Colander	2 tbsp oil
Pestle and mortar	2 tbsp coriander powder
Wok and ladle	1 tbsp cumin powder
Bamboo leaves	1 tbsp sugar
String	2 tsp salt
Large pot	200 ml water
Wooden tongs	800 g glutinous rice, soaked overnight

Method

1 Cut the pork into 1 cm cubes and place in a pot of boiling water for 1-2 minutes to part-cook. Drain.

2 In a mortar, grind the onion and garlic to a purée. Heat the oil in the wok and fry the purée for 4 minutes. Add the pork and stir-fry for 2 minutes.

3 Add the coriander, cumin powder, sugar and salt and cook for 2 minutes. Add the water and cook over a high heat until the mixture is almost dry but still moist. Transfer to a plate to cool.

4 Blanch the bamboo leaves in a pot of boiling water, then drain. Drain the soaked glutinous rice.

5 Fold one leaf in two, making a triangular container with a long back from two leaf ends. Place 1 tbsp rice onto the bamboo leaf, press on 1 tbsp of pork mixture and cover with another 1 tbsp rice. Fold over both leaf ends to make a pyramid-shaped dumpling.

6 Hold the dumpling firmly while wrapping a piece of string twice around it, and tie firmly. Leave a tail of at least 20 cm of string make it easier to remove the cooked dumplings from the pot using the tongs.

7 Bring a large pot of water to the boil, add the dumplings and simmer for 1 hour. To serve, cut the string from the dumplings and take to the table, where diners can remove the leaves themselves.

grinding implements

These pestle and mortar sets are not different merely for aesthetic reasons, each has specific purposes. Indochina's uniquely shaped terracotta model is meant for processing delicate fresh herbs and spices for salad-making. The stronger granite version is the one needed for pounding pungent curry pastes from firm fresh ingredients such as candlenuts, galangal, garlic and chillies.

1 Terracotta pestle and mortar The pestle accompanying the tall terracotta mortar is a large wooden club, about 30 cm long. It does a gentle bashing job rather than grinding foods, so is not effective for pounding hard ingredients to a paste or powder. The mortar's depth and size, however, mean that after a salad dressing has been made in it, the other salad ingredients can be tossed and turned there too, without the need for a salad bowl. Wash it in hot soapy water, then turn upside down and leave to dry before storing. Used properly, one of these will last several lifetimes.

2 Granite pestle and mortar A granite mortar can withstand the heavy pounding needed to produce fine fresh curry pastes. To use, prepare all the ingredients and place them in individual bowls, ensuring the foods are dry to the touch. Start with drier items such as candlenuts and garlic, before moving onto those that will splatter. Always grind a small amount at a time. With a regular thumping and circular motion, grind the spices on the bottom and sides of the pestle. Keep a spoon handy to scrape down the bits that rise up the sides of the pestle and, when done, use the spoon to scrape up every last bit of paste.

---

green curry with fish dumplings and aubergine

Tools	Ingredients
Cleaver	*For the fish dumplings*
Chopping board	3 coriander roots, chopped
Pestle and mortar	a pinch of salt
Large bowl	1 tbsp chopped wild ginger
Pot	5 white peppercorns
Wire mesh	200 g pike or monkfish fillets
strainer	2 tbsp fish sauce or light soy sauce
Saucepan	a little palm sugar
Spoon	1 stalk lemongrass, crushed
	For the curry
	500 ml coconut cream
	3 tbsp green curry paste
	(see page 110)
	a little chicken stock or extra
	coconut milk
	fish sauce, to taste
	chillies, to taste
	500 ml coconut milk
	3-4 apple aubergines, quartered
	2 kaffir lime leaves
	a few long green and red chillies,
	deseeded and julienned
	a handful of Thai basil
	a little shredded wild ginger

Method

1 To make the fish dumplings, in the mortar, pound the coriander roots with salt, wild ginger and peppercorns until fine in texture. Transfer to a large bowl and clean out the mortar.

2 Place the fish in the mortar and pound until smooth. Add it to the bowl and work the mixture into a ball. Pick up the ball and throw it back into the bowl. Repeat several times to develop the flavour and firm up the flesh. Season with fish sauce or light soy sauce and some palm sugar.

3 Roll and pinch portions of the fish mixture between your fingers to give dumplings of about 2 cm diameter. Bring a pot of salted water to the boil and add the crushed lemongrass. Reduce the heat and, working in batches if necessary, gently poach the dumplings for about 2 minutes. Drain and set aside.

4 Meanwhile, in a saucepan, bring the coconut cream to a boil and boil until it separates. Reduce the heat to medium and add the green curry paste. Cook for 4 minutes, adding some chicken stock if necessary, until the curry looks like scrambled eggs. Add fish sauce and chillies to taste.

5 Stir in the coconut milk and return to the boil. Add the aubergines and cook for 3 minutes. Just before serving, add the fish dumplings, kaffir lime leaves, green and red chillies, Thai basil and wild ginger.

green curry with fish dumplings and aubergine

Having first come to prominence at his former Sydney restaurant Darley Street Thai, david thompson is today recognised by the Thai government as one of the world's leading experts on Royal Thai cuisine. His knowledge is manifest in his menu at the restaurant Nahm in London's Halkin Hotel, where this mouth-watering dish features. You can use an oiler fish to make the dumplings, but will need to adjust the flavour balance of the sauce.

Serves 4
Preparation time: 30 minutes

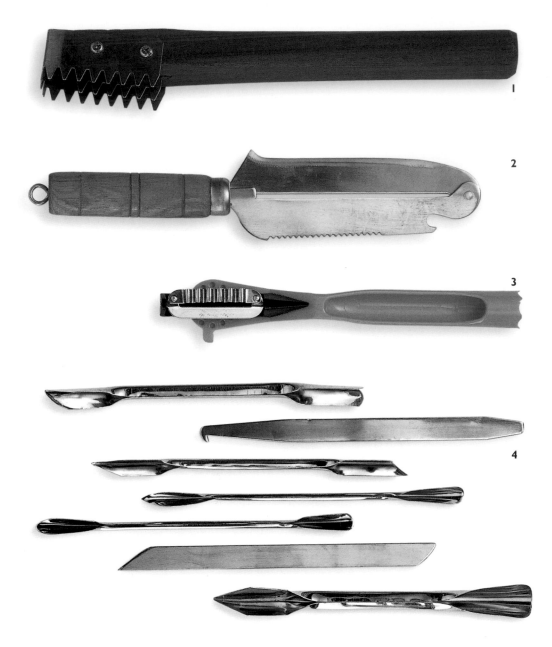

scaling, shredding and carving

Many small jobs in the Indochinese kitchen are not small in importance, as the way an ingredient is prepared has a major impact on the texture and presentation of a dish. This is most evident in Thai cooking, where salads may be given an artful touch by shredding or carving the ingredients so that the dish looks and tastes glorious. Good cooks also prefer to do their own processing of fresh seafood, and this is performed with specific tools to make the job much easier.

1 Fish scaler This simple but effective tool comprises a wooden handle attached at one end to a serrated metal blade bent into a U-shape. The sharp teeth make short work of descaling fresh fish.

2 Dual-purpose slicer and shredder Mounted on a wooden handle, this tool makes a fine job of cutting wafer-thin slices of firm fruits and vegetables, while the serrated edge is used for producing fine shreds.

3 Vegetable shredder Suitable for right- or left-handed people, this swivel-bladed gadget makes fine strands of fruits and vegetables, as well as very thin slices.

4 Fruit and vegetable carving set Looking rather like a tool kit for dentists or surgeons, this collection of specialised blades is available in various sizes in Thai stores. Once the preserve of the royal kitchens, carving fruit and vegetables into intricate floral shapes is a skill of which Thai chefs are particularly proud and the results of their labours are often found adorning lavish buffet tables. The tips of these tools may be curved, or pointed to near-needle sharpness for making the necessary nicks in melons and root vegetables, and mimicking the delicate petals of a flower. Dexterity is enhanced by holding the tools close to the blade while carving. The sharp ends may be poked into a cork for safety.

shaped cutters and moulds

The special moulds and other tools for making the bewildering range of Indochinese sweetmeats and snacks have evolved over centuries. Originally made from natural materials such as wood or bamboo, they are today available in light metals. Many are shaped to echo the symbolism rife in ancient Asian cultures, or designed to make intricate patterns of great visual beauty.

5 Long serrated cutter The jellies eaten in Indochina are not of the wobbly, gelatinous type known in Western countries. Most are firm and made from agar agar, a seaweed by-product. In Asia it is usually sold in long translucent strips, but in the West is readily available in granules. Agar agar has the advantage of being able to set without refrigeration, a real benefit in hot climates. Often enriched with coconut cream, the jellies are moulded and turned out but rarely served whole. They may be cut into diamond or triangles with a regular knife however this serrated

cutter produces slices of jelly that are then served from a plate.

6 Vegetable cutters Metal cutters such as these, shaped into Chinese characters, flowers or animals, are used to stamp out shapes from slices of carrot, radish and other hard root vegetables. The shapes are then used to decorate dishes of noodles and salads. These cutters are also commonly used in China.

7 Brass shaped cutters Strips of brass are bent into floral or heraldic cutters for little rice flour cookies.

8, 9 Turtle and fish moulds Animals, birds and plants all have their place in ritualistic practices. These moulds are probably derived from those used by European colonials in earlier times, but are now used extensively in Indochina to make a wide range of sweet puddings.

10 Tweezers Even the smallest rice flour cake will be lovingly designed and crimped to take on pretty floral forms. These tweezers, available large and small, are for pinching designs and attractive rimmed edges on cakes, cookies and pastries.

vietnamese cabbage salad

This is a crisp, refreshing salad that goes well with barbecued meats, Vietnamese spring rolls or as a light starter. The recipe comes from marlena spieler who has produced many top-selling cookbooks and is European food correspondent for the *San Francisco Chronicle*.

Serves 8-10

Preparation time: 25 minutes, plus 30 minutes sweating

Tools	Ingredients
Cleaver	1 cabbage
Chopping board	1 cucumber
Mandolin	2 carrots
Vegetable shredder	1 bunch spring onions
Large bowl	5 cloves garlic
Large sieve or colander	1-2 tbsp shredded or chopped ginger
	6 tbsp sugar
	3 tbsp white wine vinegar
	juice of 2 limes or lemons
	2-3 tbsp sesame oil
	½ tsp dried red pepper flakes or ½ chopped fresh chilli
	2 tsp light soy sauce or fish sauce
	3 tbsp chopped fresh coriander
	1 tbsp chopped fresh mint, optional
	6-8 tbsp skinned peanuts, coarsely chopped
	salt

Method

1 Core and thinly slice the cabbage, using the mandolin or cleaver. Julienne the cucumber, shred the carrots. Thinly slice the springs onions and chop the garlic.

2 In a large bowl, combine the cabbage, cucumber, carrots, green onions, garlic, ginger and salt generously. Set aside for at least 30 minutes to sweat, then drain and squeeze out the excess liquid, handfuls and a time.

3 Add all the remaining ingredients, except the peanuts, season to taste, then cover and refrigerate.

4 Before serving, drain the salad again and adjust the seasonings to taste. Serve garnished with the peanuts

grill racks

Grilled and barbecued foods figure prominently in Indochina. Everywhere in the cities and towns from Bangkok to Ho Chi Minh city, street vendors ply their wares from makeshift carts that contain no more than a charcoal brazier and various implements for grilling meats and seafoods. Racks such as these hold the food tightly yet openly, allowing the cook to baste the food liberally with marinade using a brush or a bruised stalk of lemongrass, which will add its own delicious flavour.

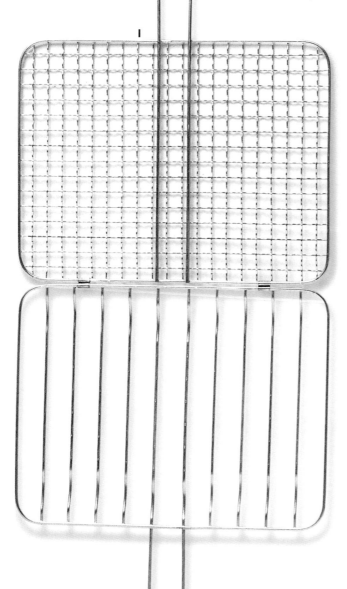

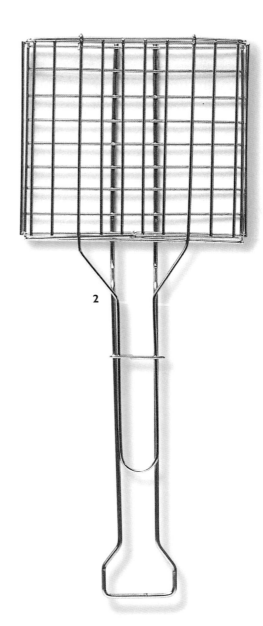

1 Large wire rack These wire racks are a modern take on rustic bamboo ones and can cradle a whole fish, spatchcocked chicken or wild bird, large squid and split jumbo prawns. The handles allow frequent turning for effective barbecuing. Because they are made of metal, the handles get extremely hot during cooking, so it is advisable to wrap a damp towel around them. After use, the racks should be scrubbed vigorously to remove stuck-on bits of charred food and stubborn stains.

2 Small wire rack This is ideal for grilling smaller items such as spiced patties and shellfish, and helps to prevent flavourings such as garlic, onions and herbs falling away.

north vietnamese fish brochettes

There was once a road in Hanoi called Phõ hàng chà cá, named in celebration of this dish, cha ca nuong, but now it has another name. Yet this recipe from seafood expert and food historian alan davidson is still among the most celebrated in North Vietnam. You can use any sea fish with firm flesh, and for authenticity choose the Vietnamese fish sauce nuoc mam.

Serves 4

Preparation time: 20 minutes, plus 2-3 hours marinating

Tools	Ingredients	Method
Cleaver	500 g fish meat	**1** Clean the fish, remove any bones and skin and cut the flesh into 3 cm cubes.
Chopping board	4 rashers streaky bacon	**2** In a large bowl, combine the ingredients for the marinade, add the cubed fish and turn gently to coat. Leave to marinate for 2-3 hours.
Large bowl	3 tbsp oil	
Bamboo skewers	2 spring onions, chopped	
Wok	5-6 tbsp peanuts, skinned	**3** Cut the bacon into 3 cm squares. Thread the skewers with alternating pieces of fish and bacon.
Small bowl	*For the marinade*	
Grill rack	3 tbsp oil	**4** Heat the oil in the wok and fry the spring onions until soft. Transfer to a small bowl and set aside.
Basting brush	3 tbsp fish sauce	
Pestle and mortar	2 tbsp rice wine	**5** Heat a barbecue. Place the skewers on the grill rack, close and place on the barbecue. Baste the fish during cooking with the onion oil.
	a pinch of turmeric	
	2 tsp chopped wild ginger	
	2 tsp shrimp paste	**6** Pound the nuts in the mortar and sprinkle them over the fish brochettes just before serving.

coconut wood tools

The coconut palm provides more than just food in the tropics. Its leaves and trunk are used in building, the hair covering the mature shells is made into matting, and the oil is made into cosmetics. Coconut shells are never without purpose in Asia and, even without being crafted into utensils, they make handy water scoops, all-purpose containers and serving bowls.

1, 5 Coconut shell ladles The natural curve of coconut shells makes them ideal ladles when a handle is attached. Similar tools are found in most coconut growing regions, including South India. The long-handled ladles are ideal for serving soups and curries, while shorter ones can be used as rice scoops, or for serving salads and desserts.

2 Perforated spoon Coconut wood may seem rustic, yet this humble material can be shaped, perforated or carved to function like any modern kitchen implement. This one is a useful straining or draining tool.

3 Spatula This tool is finely honed to work just as well as the modern equivalent for flipping and stirring.

4 Slotted spoon Like the perforated spoon, this tool is useful for lifting saucy foods from the wok.

6 Salad servers Salads are a key feature of Indochinese cuisines. Here fine craftsmanship transforms the coconut shell into a salad set comprising a large fork and spoon with smooth, rounded handles.

natural basketware

Various types of palm frond are dried and woven into a range of functional and decorative containers for food storage and presentation in Indochina. Thai and Laotian meals in particular often feature sticky rice that is served in these small baskets, and they do double duty as containers for rice crackers, prawn wafers, spiced nuts and vegetable crudités.

1 Large storage basket Made of very fine bamboo weave, square at the bottom and round at the top, this type of basket is traditionally used for storing dry grain. This is not advisable in kitchens today, as grain products should be stored in robust sealed containers to deter pests.

2 Water bucket In remote areas where modern plastic products are a rarity, large dried leaves are fashioned into buckets such as this one used for collecting fresh water.

4 Steaming basket Here a large palm basket with sloping sides sits over a metal pot. Portions of food, usually rice, are placed in the basket, the pan is filled with water, then the whole device is set over a heat source. A separate cover is put on top so that the food cooks in the steam generated in the base.

5 Small round basket Almost a replica of the Chinese rice bowl, this very fine weave basket is used for serving condiments, vegetable crudités and dry snacks.

3 Lidded basket A clever design featuring broad bands of bamboo interwoven with finer strips, this attractive basket has a lid attached by a string and stands securely on its integral cross-bar feet. In Indochina a basket such as this would be used for serving cooked rice

6, 7 Small lidded baskets A tiny variation of the taller lidded basket shown left, these are used in Thailand for serving small bites. The baskets may be plain or decoratively woven, as in the star-shaped box above, with lids entirely separate, or attached by a small cord.

southeast asia
including singapore, malaysia and indonesia

southeast asia
including singapore, malaysia and indonesia

The three countries that make up Southeast Asia are not only geographical neighbours; they also share many cultural ties. Southeast Asian cooking is a heady mix of spicy, aromatic, soy-based concoctions, liberally tweaked by cross-cultural fusion elements.

Malaysia, the Indonesian Archipelago and Singapore evolved from an ancient Sri Vijaya Hindu empire centuries before it was sacked and overtaken by the jungle, and well before the Dutch and English colonialists first laid eyes on their spice-rich promise. All three regions of Southeast Asia are places of agricultural and culinary richness, and they have several dishes in common.

The cuisine is a mélange of Indian, Chinese, Arab, Dutch, British and Thai influences, with tantalising fragrances permeating the very air. Keynote flavours include ginger, lemongrass, galangal, shallots, chillies, coriander, coconut, tamarind and the dozen and one fresh herbs that impart their delicious perfumes to Southast Asia's multitude of tasty curries and stir-fries.

Fish and shellfish are spiced with chillies, turmeric, ginger and coconut milk and steamed in banana leaves. Chicken, beef and pork are cooked in heady blends of shrimp paste, shallots, galangal, lime leaves and lemongrass. Skewers of marinated chicken are grilled over charcoal, rice is drenched with coconut milk and fragrant pandan leaves. Tapioca is grated, puréed and then baked with sweet palm syrup. Delicate wafer-thin rolls of egg and coconut batter are shaped by iron plates with intricate motifs. An endless array of spicy, savoury or sweet noodles are consumed with relish. Most of these dishes are still made in the traditional way with the tools featured in this chapter.

It is not the general practice to serve desserts after Southeast Asian meals. Many of the region's sweet specialities were originally reserved for Taoist or Buddhist rituals, or to symbolise good things within the Chinese cultural pantheon. Some have over the years become popular snacks sold throughout the year, regardless of ritual links or symbolism.

The region's mixed tapestry of culinary styles is a direct result of multicultural marriages over the centuries. In particular the combination of spices, local produce and ethnic Chinese cuisine has evolved to give a distinctive style known as Nonya cooking. The word Nonya is an amalgam of 'neo', which

means lady in Chinese, and 'hya', which means gentleman-brother; the Malay term for the community is Peranakan, which means 'born of the soil', as opposed to being born in China.

Also unique to Southeast Asia is the style of street food known as hawker cooking. Indian, Malay, Chinese, Arab and Eurasian dishes are trotted out daily on the streets of every town, city and village by itinerant food vendors. These people are a much-loved feature of the region, many working from nothing more than makeshift carts, lean-tos and baskets slung on poles hoisted on sturdy shoulders.

ABOVE: **1** fried tofu, **2** tempeh, **3** black rice, **4** yellow bean paste, **5** shrimp paste, **6** fish balls, **7** sambal, **8** coconut milk, **9** chilli sauce, **10** fish cake, **11** dried whitebait. OPPOSITE: **1** chive flowers, **2** laksa leaves, **3** galangal, **4** red onion, **5** kasturi limes, **6** gai lan, **7** red chillies, **8** garlic, **9** lemongrass, **10** pandan leaf.

But today, with urbanisation, many are relegated to covered complexes, where the authentic flavours still abound, even if the ambience is devoid of rustic charm. Food culture is fundamental to Southeast Asia, so the culinary heritage is kept alive and ever delicious, even if not outdoors.

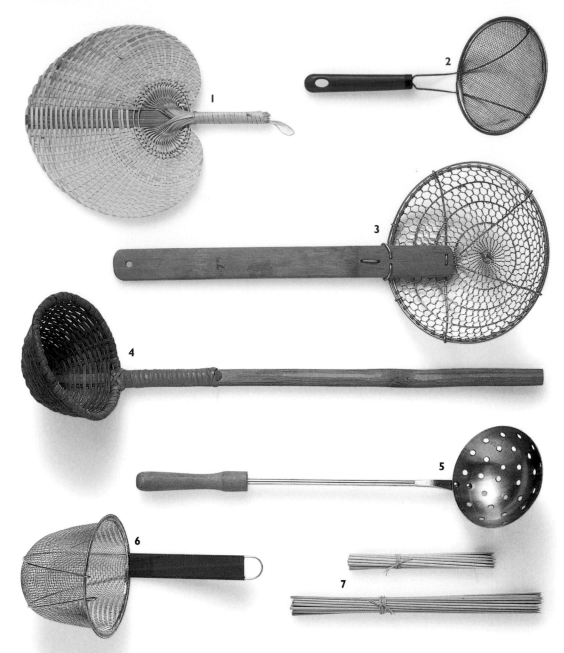

street hawker tools

Despite many Southeast Asian cities being rapidly urbanised, street hawkers remain a fascinating feature, sometimes with several family members working at the same stall. Noodles, satay, fritters and pastries, porridges of black sticky rice and coconut milk, fresh fruit cocktails and intriguing parcels of banana and pandan leaves are among the typical fare these tools help produce.

1 Woven pandan leaf fan An enduring sight in Southeast Asian streets is the mobile satay man. Given that he never knows when he will have his next customer, his charcoal brazier is ever at a ready glow. This fan, fashioned from an entire dried pandan leaf, sparks the embers of the brazier to roaring life in a few seconds. Given the humid climate and hot, smoky nature of his job, it is also used to cool the cook!

2, 6 Short handled strainers These are used for quick blanching in small or shallow pans for delicate foods like seafood and thinly sliced meats. Each requires a certain amount of dexterity, with a twist of the wrist, to blanch, shake, drain and turn out the food onto a bowl.

3, 4 Noodle strainers Before metal and plastic became the basic materials for strainers in Southeast Asia, bamboo was the mainstay. Many street hawkers in rural areas still use the implements of old, while others prefer modern wire models. Long handles are practical and safest for blanching noodles in deep pots of scalding, bubbling water.

5 Perforated ladle This handy tool is for scooping froth and pieces of blanched food from pots.

7 Bamboo skewers Usually between 16 cm and 20 cm long, these sharp bamboo skewers are used to spear small pieces of meat or seafood for grilling. It is advisable to soak them in cold water before use to minimise scorching on the grill. In Indonesia and Malaysia, larger bamboo stakes are fashioned into gripping forks that hold a whole bird for grilling. Small slivers are also used to secure leaf containers during cooking.

fried vermicelli xiamen-style

Xiamen-style indicates that this crisp noodle dish is in the manner of those from the eastern province of Fujian in China. A key characteristic is to combine seafood and meat or chicken in the same dish. This version comes from hong sai choi of the Furama Hotel, Singapore.

Serves 2-4

Preparation time: 30 minutes

Tools	Ingredients
Cleaver	100 g beansprouts
Chopping board	oil for deep-frying
Small pot	100 g rice vermicelli noodles
Bamboo strainer	150 g chicken breast fillet,
2 woks	thinly sliced
Wok ladle	125 g raw prawns, deveined
Wire strainer	80 g green bell pepper, sliced
	80 g red bell pepper, sliced
	1 chicken stock cube
	½ tsp oyster sauce
	a pinch of sugar
	½ tsp sesame oil

Method

1 In a pot of boiling water, blanch the beansprouts for 1 minute, then drain and set aside.

2 In a wok, heat the oil for deep-frying until smoking and fry the vermicelli a handful at a time until golden and puffed. Lift out the cooked vermicelli with a wire strainer and set aside.

3 Remove all but 2 tbsp of oil from the wok. Stir-fry the chicken and prawns in it for 3 minutes until cooked. Remove and set aside.

4 Stir-fry the bell peppers for 1 minute, then add the chicken, prawns, beansprouts, stock cube, oyster sauce, sugar and sesame oil and stir-fry for 1 minute.

5 Briefly reheat the vermicelli in a separate wok for about 1 minute, spoon the sauce over and serve.

tools for edible baskets

Asian chefs have always been at the cutting edge when it comes to presentation skills. With ingenuity being the mother of invention, many 'plates' at banquets and other festive occasions are actually edible cradles made using the special tools featured here. Such tricks are not restricted to professional chefs either. In Southeast Asia, few home kitchens are without the pietee maker, which looks like a miniature golf putting club, and housewives are adept at creating diminutive cups of pastry or 'top hats' with them to be filled with all manner of cooked ingredients.

1 Pietee maker This tool comprises a heavy knob of brass with smooth grooves, attached to an L-shaped metal bar. The knob is dipped into boiling oil and then into batter, to be popped back into the oil to deep-fry into little baskets. When done to a crisp turn, the baskets come away easily from the mould. The resulting cups are shaped exactly like little top hats, then filled with cooked bamboo shoots and other fillings and served as amusing starters or canapés called kueh pietee in the

local dialect. The story goes that they were little finger food items for parties, hence the patois translation of 'pietee'. The term 'kueh' refers to all kinds of cakes, snacks and sweetmeats. It needs practice to make perfect cups and if the temperature is not right, you end up with bottomless cups! However, the advantage is that you can make the cups way ahead of serving time and store them in an airtight container for up to a month. Never wash these moulds with detergents as the soapy suds may linger in the joint between the knob and the bar. Just wipe clean with a kitchen towel after cooking and store in a cool, dry place.

2 Lompang mould Also known as a flower mould, this Indonesian tool features a flower-shaped ring attached to a thin metal rod. It is dipped in sweet batter of rice flour, sugar and coconut milk, then into hot oil to make cakes called Kueh Lompang or Swaying Flower Cakes as they are light enough to flutter in a stiff breeze.

3, 4, 5 Basket moulds The 'basket' referred to here is actually made of strips of yam, potato or noodles, arranged in such a way that when deep-fried, they produce little edible bowls that can then be used to contain various stir-fried ingredients. The traditional model comprises two large perforated ladles shaped to fit one inside the other. The handles are of bamboo or wood set at a right angle to the bowls. Strips of yam or sweet potato are first dusted with cornflour or tapioca flour, then laid into the larger ladle to form a kind of nest. The smaller ladle is then used to press down firmly on this nest. The flour acts as a binder and, when deep-fried, these baskets hold their shape firmly. The modern version is much like a pair of wire mesh sieves held together by a hinge. Also available are perforated models without handles. These float freely in the hot oil during cooking; they are more difficult to use as there is nothing to help press the basket ingredients together while in the oil.

making edible baskets

Cut the vegetable strips as thinly as possible (left) so that they are pliable enough to sit easily in the mould (right). There should be no visible gaps between the strips at the base of the mould. A thorough dusting of cornflour helps the strips to seal properly. For an attractive brim, allow 4 cm above the top of the mould (bottom). Yam is preferred for its starchy, crisp texture and delicious flavour. Cheaper potatoes can also be used; they need to be long enough to yield strips of 10-12 cm.

prawns in yam basket

An impressive dish for dinner parties, this spectacular basket filled with succulent stir-fried prawns is easier than it looks, especially when you have the right tools for the job. Gently swirling the yam basket around in the oil a little while deep-frying will help it to brown nicely.

Serves 4

Preparation time: 30 minutes

Tools	Ingredients
Cleaver	1 large yam, cut into fine strips
Chopping board	4 tbsp cornflour
Yam basket mould	oil for deep-frying
Wok and ladle	salad leaves, to garnish
	For the filling
	3 tbsp oil
	2 cloves garlic, crushed
	1 small carrot, cubed
	1 stalk celery, sliced
	20 button mushrooms
	400 g jumbo prawns, shelled with tails left on
	2 tbsp sesame oil
	1 tsp black pepper
	1 tbsp ginger juice
	2 tbsp oyster sauce
	1 tbsp cornflour

Method

1 Toss the strips of yam in the cornflour. Lay them in the lower ladle of mould, overlapping slightly. Press firmly with the upper ladle.

2 Heat the oil in the wok and fry the basket until crisp and golden.

3 Gently lift the mould out of the oil and prise the yam basket loose. Place it on a serving dish that has been dressed with leaves.

4 To make the filling, heat the oil in the cleaned wok and stir-fry the garlic for 1 minute. Add the carrot, celery and mushrooms and stir-fry for 2 minutes. Add the prawns, sesame oil, pepper, ginger juice and oyster sauce and continue cooking for a further 5 minutes.

5 Blend the cornflour with a little water and add it to the wok. Stir until the sauce thickens. Transfer to the yam basket and serve.

top hats

Crispy little cups of feather-light fried batter, these exotic 'vol au vents' are unique to Southeast Asia where they are known as kueh pietee. Filled with a savoury mixture of yam beans and bamboo strips, they make delightful appetisers or finger food for parties.

Makes 40
Preparation time: 1 hour

Tools	Ingredients	Method
Cleaver	*For the batter*	**1** To make the filling, peel the yam bean or swede and cut into fine julienne about 3 cm long. Do the same with the bamboo shoots.
Chopping board	300 g plain flour	
Wok and ladle	600 ml water	
Vegetable shredder	1 tsp salt	**2** Heat the oil in the wok and fry the crushed garlic for 2 minutes. Add the preserved yellow beans and mash lightly with the wok ladle. Add the julienne vegetables and stir-fry for 2 minutes. Add the soy sauce and water, bring to a boil over a high heat, and boil for 10 minutes. Turn the heat down to medium and simmer for 20 minutes or until almost dry.
Large bowl	3 eggs	
Small bowl	oil for deep-frying	
Sieve	*For the filling*	
Small, deep pot	200 g Chinese yam bean	
Pietee mould	or swedes	
Small, deep cup	400 g bamboo shoots, canned	
Long chopsticks	4 tbsp oil	**3** Meanwhile, to make the batter, put the flour in a bowl and make a well in the centre. Add the water a little at a time, mixing into a batter the consistency of pouring cream. Add the salt and stir well.
	4 cloves garlic, crushed	
	3 tbsp preserved yellow beans	
	3 tbsp dark soy sauce	**4** Break the eggs into a separate bowl and beat lightly. Add them to the batter, stirring until well incorporated. Strain through a sieve and chill for 1 hour.
	500 ml water	
	fresh coriander leaves, to garnish	**5** Heat the oil for deep-frying in a small pot, making sure the depth of oil is greater than the depth of the pietee mould. Place some of the batter in a small, deep cup. When dipped, the base of the mould should not be able to touch the bottom of the pot or the cup, otherwise the delicate batter will smear.
	chilli sauce, to serve	

6 When the oil is smoking hot, immerse the mould in it for at least 5 minutes to heat thoroughly. Lift the mould out and gently shake off the excess oil.

7 Dip the mould quickly and without quivering into the batter, making sure you do not dip the mould in beyond its rim or the resulting fried cup will be 'locked' onto it.

8 Dip the coated mould into the hot oil. Within 1-2 minutes, the batter will turn light brown. When it is golden brown, lift out the mould and gently prise the cup off using chopsticks. Set aside to drain while you cook the remaining cups.

9 To serve, place about 2 tsp of the warm filling into each cup and top with fresh coriander. Serve with chilli sauce.

pots and pans

The wok is the favoured pan for everyday cooking in Southeast Asia. But other types of pot receive frequent use, not only in making specialities but also common dishes such as soups. Pressure cookers speed up cooking of key staples, and in households of Chinese descent the steamboat is a very popular form of communal cooking and eating.

3 Electric steamboat Today's electric steamboat is related to the ancient Mongolian firepot used in China and Korea. The modern versions are cleaner and safer to use than the traditional charcoal-fired models, but lack rustic appeal. Steamboats are used in several parts of Asia; typical ingredients differ according to available ingredients and favourite local dipping sauces. In Thailand a spicy tom yam version is produced, while the Sichuanese steamboat is flavoured with chillies and at one time included poppy heads.

1 Pressure cooker This is an indispensable utensil for a number of dishes that require long, slow cooking without the attendant reduction of liquids. Braised belly pork in five-spice powder, beef rendang and green mung beans in coconut milk, for example, take less than half the normal time to cook when made in a pressure cooker. It also eliminates the need for pre-soaking when cooking local staple foods such as soy beans and black sticky rice.

2 Double-boiler This modern version of the old Chinese utensil is used for slow simmering and stewing. The water boils in the aluminium base, conducting steam heat to the upper porcelain container. It can be used for custards and other eggy mixtures, slow-cooked herbal stews such as chicken with ginseng, and soups containing delicate ingredients.

4 Wire mesh spoons Brass or aluminium wire mesh individual spoons are specially made for dunking raw foods into the steamboat. Each diner is given one in which to place preferred foods for cooking. It is a unique way of cooking to a desired consistency or doneness and prevents portions floating around and getting overcooked. When all the food is eaten, the resulting broth is usually very rich from all the different flavours of meat, poultry, seafood and vegetables that have been cooked in these spoons.

5, 6 Simmering pots Southeast Asian households have a range of quality pots and saucepans to do jobs that the wok does not do well, such as blanching, soup- and stock-making and cooking noodles and congee. Nonstick models are useful to prevent scorching.

steamboat

The last word in tabletop cooking, the steamboat is both a festive meal and a heart-warming way to entertain. The work is solely in the preparation of raw ingredients; these can be anything you like as long as they are sliced into bite-sized pieces. A rich stock is made from either chicken bones or stock cubes and then transferred to the moat of the steamboat. Traditionally, the stock is heated by charcoal lit under the moat; electric models are also available. Diners help themselves to whatever they fancy, and cook the food pieces to suit their own taste.

Serves 10-14
Preparation time: 45 minutes

Tools	Ingredients	Method
Large pot	4 litres chicken stock	**1** Bring the stock to a boil in a large pot. Meanwhile, cut all the ingredients into bite-sized pieces and arrange them on presentation plates.
Cleaver	400 g lean pork fillet	
Chopping board	400 g beef fillet	
Steamboat	400 g chicken breast	**2** Pour the stock in the steamboat, place on the table and light or switch on. Take the food to the table and set around the steamboat. Provide little dishes of light soy sauce, chilli sauce, mustard and pepper for individuals to season the cooked food to taste.
Wire mesh spoons	500 g tiger prawns, peeled	
	20 fishballs	
	200 g pig's liver *(optional)*	
	200 g squid	
	400 g tofu	**3** When the stock begins to bubble, each guest places their food of choice into the wire mesh spoons, and lays them in the stock to cook.
	100 g transparent vermicelli, soaked until soft	
	1 Chinese cabbage	**4** At the end of the meal the stock will be incredibly rich and can be served as a broth.
	light soy sauce, chilli sauce, mustard and pepper, to serve	

beef rendang

This dish moves from boiling to frying in a continuous process, says writer and cookery teacher sri owen, who is the author of several highly regarded works including *Indonesian Regional Food and Cookery* and *The Rice Book*. 'As the water in the coconut milk is driven off, the oil remains, until eventually the meat has absorbed the oil and has become almost black, quite dry but richly succulent, while the solid residue from the oil forms a kind of dry relish.' Brisket is the cut of beef Sri recommends for this dish, but silverside or stewing steak are also suitable.

Serves 6-8

Preparation time: 1 hour

Tools	Ingredients	Method
Cleaver	5 shallots	**1** Peel and slice the shallots finely, and roughly chop the chillies, garlic and ginger. Process them all with the pestle and mortar until fine.
Chopping board	6 red chillies or 3 tsp chilli powder	
Pestle and mortar	4 cloves garlic	**2** Place all the ingredients in a pressure cooker and cook for about 1 hour.
Pressure cooker	2.5 cm fresh ginger, peeled	
Ladle	1.5 kg brisket, cut into	**3** Release the pressure by running the cooker under a cold tap, then open the lid and stir well. The coconut milk will have rendered down to be mostly oil.
	2 cm strips or cubes	
	1 tsp turmeric powder	
	1 tsp chopped galangal or	**4** Return the pan to the heat, uncovered, and fry the rendang for about 15 minutes until the coconut oil has become thick and brown. Serve with rice.
	½ tsp galangal powder	
	2.3 litres coconut milk	
	1 bay leaf	
	1 fresh turmeric leaf or	
	1 stalk lemongrass	
	2 tsp salt	

nonya-style pork curry

Penang, where this dish called pork gulai originated, was once the northern Malaysian enclave for the Straits Chinese community, known as Babas and Nonyas. The term 'gulai' is Penang patois for any kind of curry or sambal. This recipe comes from neil perry, a leading Australian chef.

Serves 10

Preparation time: 45 minutes

Tools	Ingredients	Method

Tools
Cleaver
Chopping board
Pestle and mortar
Steamer
Large pot

Ingredients
5 tbsp coriander seeds
2 tsp fennel seeds
1.25 kg pumpkin
1.25 kg pork shoulder
10 cloves garlic
2 Spanish onions, chopped
10 cm fresh turmeric, chopped
8 fresh long red chillies,
  deseeded, chopped
10 dried chillies,
  soaked in warm water
100 ml oil
1 stalk lemongrass
250 ml coconut cream
2 star anise
5 cloves
5 cm stick cinnamon
salt and pepper

Method
1 In a dry pan, toast the coriander and fennel seeds separately until fragrant, then grind in the mortar.
2 Peel the pumpkin, cut into large chunks and steam for 20 minutes until cooked but still firm.
3 Meanwhile, cut the pork into bite-sized chunks. Grind the garlic, onion, turmeric, fresh and dried chillies, and the coriander and fennel to a paste.
4 Heat the oil in a pot. Bruise the lemongrass and fry for 30 seconds before adding the spice paste. Fry over low heat for 4 minutes.
5 Stir in the coconut cream, star anise, cloves and cinnamon. Then add the pork, mix well and cook for about 30 minutes or until the meat is tender.
6 Add the steamed pumpkin for the last 5 minutes of cooking, and salt and pepper to taste.

tools for cakes and snacks

In Southeast Asia cakes and cookies are traditionally associated with symbolism and festive rites, especially during Taoist festivals. Those that originated in China are still held in reverence for their Yin-Yang symbolism. Others evolved from a blend of Indonesian, Malay and Chinese cultures.

4 Cookie moulds This is for small cakes known as kueh koyah. They are made of mung bean flour and usually feature leaf or fruit motifs. Plastic models are also available.

5 Curry puff mould Curry puffs, the half-moon-shaped Anglo-Indian pasties with crimped edges, were traditionally shaped by hand, but this fold-over plastic mould makes the job easier, neater and faster.

6 Round cutter Rings of aluminium in various sizes are used to stamp out rounds of pastry and dough.

7 Brass crimper and roller This clever double-ended tool is for decorating and shaping crumbly cookies of rice and coconut milk.

8 Melon baller Shown here is a heart-shaped version of a melon baller. In Southeast Asia, melon balls are often served piled up in large fruit shells, or added to sweet drinks, and sometimes used as a filling for rice and wheat flour cakes, instead of red bean paste.

9 Boat-shaped tart mould Looking like little aluminium boats, these moulds are used for the pastry base of pineapple and fruit tarts, usually served during Chinese New Year.

10 Grooved metal tart mould This oval mould contains an inset piece of wood for shaping pastry cases. It stamps each case to give a raised rim and mashed pineapple is then piled inside for baking.

1, 3 Longevity cake moulds Paisley or round templates are carved from wooden blocks, featuring motifs symbolic of long life and prosperity.

2 Mooncake mould Mooncakes are made of rice flour dough and filled with sweet almond or mung bean mash, pressed into the mould, gently knocked out and steamed or baked. The moulds are made of hardwood and carved with designs symbolic of the moon and its role in mythology.

curry puffs

These Malaysian snacks look like small Cornish pasties and are usually filled with a curried potato and chicken or lamb mixture. They are believed to have evolved during colonial days when British expatriates and rubber plantation owners, missing their traditional pasties, asked their cooks to come up with something similar containing meat and potato. Given that most cooks in those days were indentured workers from Southern India, spices were usually featured in cooking, so Malaysia created a nice fusion-style curried pastie. If you do not wish to make your own dough, use 400 g of ready-made shortcrust pastry.

Makes 20
Preparation time: 35 minutes

Tools

Chopping board
Cleaver
Large bowl
Small rolling pin
7 cm cookie cutter
Wok and ladle
Curry puff mould
Wire mesh strainer

Ingredients

For the dough
300g plain flour,
   plus extra for dusting
a pinch of salt
60 g butter or margarine
70 ml water
For the filling
2 tbsp curry powder
1 tbsp oil,
   plus extra for deep-frying
2 cloves garlic, crushed
300 g minced lamb
150 g potato,
   peeled and finely diced
1 tsp salt
1 tsp sugar

Method

1 To make the pastry, mix the flour and salt in a bowl and rub in the butter to give a crumbly texture. Add the water and knead well until the dough comes away from the bowl. Roll out the pastry to 3 mm thick and cut out circles with the cookie cutter. Set aside.

2 Mix the curry powder with 2 tbsp water to make a paste. Heat 1 tbsp oil in the wok and fry the crushed garlic until light brown. Add the curry paste and stir over low heat for a few minutes without letting it burn.

3 Add the meat and potato. Stir until the meat is cooked and the mixture is moist but not watery. Mix in the salt and sugar, then leave to cool.

4 Place a circle of pastry in the curry puff mould and add 1 tbsp of the meat mixture. Close to seal the edges, giving a half-moon-shaped parcel with crimped edges. Repeat with the remaining dough circles.

5 Clean out the wok and heat some oil in it for deep-frying. Cook the curry puffs until golden brown. Drain on kitchen paper before serving.

longevity cakes

The Chinese name of ang ku kueh is translated to 'red turtle cakes' for two reasons. Red is symbolic of prosperity, and the turtle of longevity. Each mould is usually etched with the design of a turtle or a Chinese character for prosperity and the cake is dyed red for good measure.

Serves 6
Preparation time: 1 hour, plus overnight soaking

Tools	Ingredients
Cleaver	200 g sweet potato, diced
Chopping board	400 g glutinous rice flour
Saucepans	300 ml coconut milk
Colander	3 tbsp sugar
Mixing bowl	a pinch of salt
Steamer	½ tsp cochineal red colouring
Longevity cake moulds	*For the filling*
Banana leaves	500 g shelled mung beans, soaked overnight
	200 ml water
	500 g sugar

Method

1 In a small pan, simmer the sweet potato in enough water to cover for 5 minutes, then drain and mash well with a fork. Mix with half the glutinous rice flour, half the coconut milk, and the sugar and salt.

2 Bring the remaining coconut milk to a slow simmer and mix with the remaining glutinous rice flour. Stir well to give a thick dough.

3 Combine both doughs and knead on a floured board for 5 minutes. Add the colouring and knead to incorporate thoroughly.

4 To make the filling, drain the soaked beans into a steamer tray and cook for 15 minutes or until very soft. Mash well.

5 Place the water and sugar in a pan and boil to give a thick syrup. Add the mashed beans and cook over a low heat until the mixture is very dry and thick. Set aside to cool.

6 Oil the palms of your hands and divide the dough into lemon-sized balls. Flatten a little, then make a deep dent in the centre of the dough and fill with 1 tbsp of the bean filling (top left). Close up and seal.

7 Press the filled ball into a mould (centre) and apply gentle pressure so that the design of the mould is deeply etched on the surface of the cake when turned out (bottom).

8 Soak the banana leaves in hot water and cut into squares slightly larger than the cakes. Place a cake on each square, place in the steamer and cook for 15 minutes. Serve cold.

tools for cakes and snacks

Some of the most distinctive sweetmeats of Southeast Asia have transcended their festive and symbolic roles to become everyday snacks sold by street hawkers, restaurants and gourmet retailers. Such is their popularity that traditional moulds have been given high-tech treatment. Once in danger of becoming extinct, these now take pride of place in the region's culinary cultures.

1, 2 Kueh bolu moulds These moulds make little egg-based sponge cakes known as kueh bolu. The traditional model is brass or copper, with a lid designed to contain hot charcoal on top while the mould itself is heated on a clay oven. The modern version is much the same but runs on electricity. The moulds are shaped with floral and animal motifs symbolic of luck or prosperity, or simply to look pretty for festive occasions.

3, 4 Love letter moulds Kueh blander or love letters are traditional egg rolls, wafer-thin and crisp, that originated in China but are now made mainly in Southeast Asia. The moulds were made of iron, and featured two plates etched with heraldic designs clasped tightly together and attached to long handles for manipulating over a charcoal brazier. The modern electric version looks like a waffle-maker. The word 'blander' refers to a genus of crabs that mate for life and are always found in pairs in coastal areas of Malaysia. The belief is that the cakes were originally made to hide secret messages between lovers, and warring factions.

little sponge cakes

The name of these charming festive cakes, kueh bolu, literally means 'round cakes', not on account of their shape but in homage to the moon. Once reserved for Chinese New Year, kueh bolu are now eaten all year round thanks to the ease with which they can be made in the modern electric moulds. These cakes are easy to produce, but for best results it is essential to beat the eggs with an electric whisk until the mixture is white and frothy.

Serves 4
Preparation time: 40 minutes

Tools	Ingredients
Large bowl	6 eggs
Electric whisk	140 g sugar
Pestle and mortar	50 g plain flour
Electric kueh bolu mould	a pinch of salt
Pastry brush	4 tbsp coconut milk
	2 pandan leaves

Method

1 Crack the eggs into a large bowl. Add the sugar and salt and beat with an electric whisk until the mixture is white and frothy.
2 Stir in the flour and coconut milk and blend to give a smooth batter.
3 Grind the pandan leaves with the pestle to extract the liquid essence, then strain into the egg mixture.
4 Heat the kueh bolu machine and thoroughly oil each mould with a pastry brush. Pour a little batter into each mould to fill to just below the rim (top picture) as the cakes will swell a little when cooked.
5 Clamp down the lid and cook until the cakes are light brown, about 3 minutes. Allow to cool before removing each cake gently from the machine with a pair of chopsticks (bottom picture). The little sponge cakes will keep for a few weeks in an airtight tin.

serving items

Meals throughout Southeast Asia are communal, served simply on banana leaves and ordinary plates and bowls. For special occasions such as weddings and birthdays, however, presentation becomes spectacular, with glorious colourful bamboo baskets to hold bulky items. The preserved fruits and sweetmeats traditionally served at Chinese New Year and Taoist festivals are presented in smaller decorated baskets, many exquisitely crafted to please the various deities.

1 Painted baskets Traditional painted baskets of woven bamboo called sia na were used for containing gifts during weddings in earlier times. Some of these could be large enough to hold bottles of wine, syrups, and whole suckling pigs, fruits and the like. Smaller ones were used for cakes and candy, carried by members of the groom's family to the bride's home on the important day, to sweeten their thoughts and lives. Much of this craft is now dying but with ingenuity, the same designs have been cast in porcelain for the same functions. Some baskets are single-tiered, others are stacked two or three high. They make ideal serving utensils for snacks and side dishes such as prawn crackers, fried shallots, peanut wafers and other titbits.

2 Porcelain banana leaf rice plate Banana leaves were traditionally used as disposable plates throughout Southeast Asia. Rural Indonesians and Malaysians still eat from leaves and other natural containers, and in more urbanised areas banana leaves are still very much associated with meal presentation, often used to line serving and dining plates, especially for festive and other special occasion dishes. They bring a colourfully rustic touch to any Sotheast Asian meal, and are used in South India too. Today you can also find these porcelain versions in good tableware outlets.

3 Lacquered stacking basket Throughout Southeast Asia, basketry remains a fundamental element in the home. As well as serving a purpose, baskets are also often fine *objets d'art*, like this multi-tiered model meant to contain sweets and candies for festive occasions.

Cutlery *(not shown)* The standard place setting for most Southeast Asian meals served with rice would be a dinner plate, fork and spoon, the cutlery usually of stainless steel or local materials such as horn or brass. To the surprise of many non-Asian people, chopsticks are not a key player in this region, being used only when noodles are served. The knife, as used in the West, never makes a show on Asian tables as it is considered a chef's tool, and too barbaric to used at the table. Nor does it serve any purpose in traditional meals, as no Asian dish requires food to be cut up at the table – all ingredients are cut into bite-sized pieces during preparation. If a soup is served during a meal, whether it is presented in individual bowls or in a large bowl placed at the centre of the table, a porcelain spoon and rest would be provided.

nasi lemak with hot chilli sambal, wok-fried eggs, whitebait and peanuts

Nasi lemak began as a hawker dish many decades ago when a simple portion of coconut rice would be wrapped in a banana leaf and flavoured with a thick, hot sambal. Today it is a veritable smorgasbord of delicious proportions and may include a curry, pickles, prawn crackers, omelette and fried fish as well as the sambal. Together, the result is more than the sum of its parts and is typically served for breakfast. Below is a recipe for coconut rce and a few classic accompaniments. The whitebait used is not fresh but a dried product called 'ikan billis' sold in most Chinese and Southeast Asian shops. The fried tamarind-marinated mackerel opposite can be included as part of the meal, alternatively you could serve a beef stew or chicken curry instead.

coconut rice
Wash 400 g jasmine rice and soak in water for 30 minutes. Drain and place on a steamer tray. Wash and tie 2 pandan leaves into knots and press them down into the rice. Pour in 400 ml coconut milk and 1 tsp salt and mix well. Place in a steamer and cook for 15 minutes. To serve, place on a banana leaf-covered plate, and top with egg and sambal; serve some sliced cucumber and other side dishes in baskets or small plates.

hot chilli sambal
Using a pestle and mortar, grind 1 large onion, 3 cloves garlic, 4 fresh red chillies and 2 tsp shrimp paste until fine. Heat 4 tbsp oil in a wok and fry the spice paste over a low heat until fragrant. Add 1 tbsp tomato purée, 2 tbsp tamarind paste, 1 tsp salt, 1 tsp sugar and continue cooking for 1 minute. When the mixture is thick and aromatic, transfer it to a bowl and set aside to cool.

wok-fried eggs
Place 4 eggs in a saucepan of cold water, bring to the boil and simmer for 6 minutes. Drain and cool under cold running water, then remove the shells. In a clean wok, heat 1 tbsp oil, add the eggs and roll them around the pan until a bown skin forms. Cut in half before serving, topping with the sambal if desired.

fried whitebait and peanuts
Shake off any excess grit from 200 g dried whitebait or ikan bilis. Heat 3 tbsp oil in a wok and stir-fry the whitebait for 4 minutes until brown and crisp. Remove from the wok and set aside. Add 200 g shelled, skinned peanuts to the wok, toss to brown lightly and serve alongside, or mixed with, the fish.

fried tamarind-marinated mackerel

A faithful companion to coconut rice, these mackerel pieces are first steeped in tamarind paste, drained and fried until crisp to give a dish known as ikan goreng asam. The sweet flesh of the mackerel takes on a special flavour when served with hot chilli sambal. Like any food with a tamarind coating, the fish will turn dark brown when fried — do not worry, this is normal.

Serves 4
Preparation time: 25 minutes

Tools	Ingredients
Cleaver	1 large mackerel, about 600 g
Chopping board	2 tbsp tamarind paste
Mixing bowl	150 ml water
Wok and ladle	1 tbsp light soy sauce
Draining rack	oil for deep-frying

Method

1 Cut the mackerel into four thick steaks, discarding the head and tail fin.
2 In a bowl, blend the tamarind paste with the water and soy sauce, add the fish and marinate for 10 minutes.
3 Heat some oil for deep-frying in a wok. Drain the fish and pat dry with kitchen paper.
4 Deep-fry the fish for about 4 minutes, turning once during cooking.
5 Drain on the rack, then serve alone with sambal, or as a part of a nasi lemak meal.

coconut egg jam

The importing of European jams to Southeast Asia during colonial times must have triggered the desire for sweet spreads for bread. Given that coconuts abound in the region, it was only a matter of time before this delicious coconut and egg jam was born. Called kaya in the Malay language, its incredible richness best explains the name, which means 'rich', as in wealthy.

Serves 10

Preparation time: 3 hours

Tools	Ingredients
2 large bowls	20 eggs
Chopsticks	750 ml coconut milk
Fine sieve	500 g sugar
Double boiler	4 pandan leaves, tied into knots
Ladle	

Method

1 Crack the eggs into a bowl and beat lightly with chopsticks. Pour through a fine sieve into another clean bowl, then sieve a second time.

2 Add the coconut milk and sugar and stir gently for 30 minutes until the sugar has almost dissolved.

3 Transfer the mixture to the double boiler and fill the bottom container two-thirds full with water. Cover and bring to the boil.

4 Using the ladle, stir the mixture slowly but continuously for 15 minutes. Rest for 15 minutes, stir for 15 minutes, then rest again and continue this pattern until the mixture is thick and glossy, about 2 hours. Halfway through cooking, add the pandan leaves.

5 Transfer the kaya to a bowl and leave to cool. Cover to store and serve with toast or bread.

134 southeast asia

suppliers

The following list incorporates sources of the equipment featured in the photographs in this book, as well as other useful suppliers of Asian kitchenware and ingredients including retailers, importers, markets, and wholesalers.

united kingdom

CHINESE, JAPANESE
AND SOUTHEAST ASIAN
Oriental City Supermarket
399 Edgware Road, Colindale, London
Tel: 020 8200 0009
Web: www.oriental-city.com

CHINESE
Hoo Hing
North Circular Road
London NW10
Tel: 020 8838 3388
Web: www.hoohing.com

New Loon Moon
9a Gerrard Street
London W1
Tel: 020 7734 3887

Wing Yip
395 Edgware Road
Cricklewood, London
Tel: 020 8452 1478
Web: www.wingyip.com

JAPANESE
Japan Centre
212 Piccadilly
London W1
Tel: 020 7434 4218
Web: www.japancentre.com

The Japanese Knife Company
Tel: 0870 240 2248
Web: www.japaneseknifecompany.com

Nippon Kitchen
Tel: 020 8881 1719
Web: www.nipponkitchen.com

Utsuwa No Yakata Tajimi UK Ltd
Oriental City
399 Edgware Road
Colindale, London
Tel: 020 8201 3002

KOREAN
Song's Supermarket
76-78 Burlington Road
New Malden, Surrey
Tel: 020 8942 8471
e-mail: css22@hotmail.com

INDIAN
Daman's Collection Ltd
36 South Road
Southhall, Middlesex

Mita Emporium
80 The Green
Southhall, Middlesex
Tel: 020 8571 6571

Quality Foods
South Road
Southall, Middlesex
Tel: 020 8917 9188

Taj Stores
112-114 Brick Lane
London E1
Tel: 020 7377 0061
Web: www.cuisinenet.co.uk/tajstores

Teendeep
30 Ealing Road
Wembley, London
Tel: 020 8903 8598

THAI
Kalimantan
The Livery Stables Market
Chalk Farm Road
Camden Town, London
Tel: 020 7482 3595

Talad Thai
326 Upper Richmond Road
Putney, London
Tel: 020 8789 8084

Tawana Supermarket
18 Chepstow Road
Notting Hill, London
Tel: 020 7221 6316

Thairama Ltd
16-18 London Road
Guildford, Surrey
Tel: 01483 536092
e-mail: thairama_uk@hotmail.com

GENERAL
Cucina Direct
Tel: 020 8246 4311
Web: www.cucinadirect.co.uk

Divertimenti
33-34 Marylebone High Street
London W1
Tel: 020 7935 0689
Web: www.divertimenti.co.uk

Habitat
196 Tottenham Court Road
London W1
Tel: 020 7631 3880
Web: www.habitat.net

House of Fraser
318 Oxford Street
London W1
Tel: 0207 529 4700
Web: www.houseoffraser.co.uk

John Lewis
Oxford Street
London W1
Tel: 020 7629 7711
Web: www.johnlewis.com

Kitchen Ideas
70 Westbourne Grove
Bayswater, London
Tel: 020 7229 3388

Kitchens Catering Utensils
4-5 Quiet Street
Bath, North East Somerset
Tel: 01225 330 524

Lakeland Ltd
Alexandra Buildings
Windemere, Cumbria
Tel: 015394 88100
Web: www.lakelandlimited.com

Selfridges
400 Oxford Street
London W1
Tel: 020 7629 1234
Web: www.selfridges.co.uk

Fox Run Craftsmen
Fox House
Stonedale Road
Stonehouse, Gloucestershire
Tel: 01453 828 333

I Grundwerg Ltd
Silversteel House
29-49 Rockingham Street
Sheffield
Tel: 0114 2756700

Imperial International
Sheene Road
Beaumont Leys
Leicester
Tel: 0116 291 9999
Web: www.imperialint.com

Typhoon Europe Ltd
Oakcroft Road
Chessington, Surrey
Tel: 0208 974 4750
e-mail: info@typhooneurope.com
Web: www.typhooneurope.com

William Levene Ltd
167 Imperial Drive
Harrow, Middlesex
Tel: 020 8868 4355

asia

Lau Choy Seng
23/25 Temple Street
Singapore 058568
Tel: 0065 6223 5486
e-mail sales@lauchoyseng.com

Rishi Handicrafts
58 Arab Street,
Singapore 199755
Tel: 065 6298 5927

Sia Huat
7-11 Temple Street
Singapore 058559
Tel: 0065 6223 1732
e-mail: enquiry@siahuat.com.sg
Web: www.siahuat.com.sg

Tang's Department Store
310-320 Orchard Road
Singapore 238864
Tel: 0065 6737 5500
Web: www.tangs.com

Yue Hwa Chinese Emporium
70 Eu Tong Sen Street
Singapore
Tel: 0065 6538 4222

Hocatsu (M) Sdn. Bhd.
6, Jalan SS 21/35 Damansara Utama,
47400 Petaling Jaya
Selangor Darul Ehsan
Tel: 00603 7725 4588
e-mail: hocatsu@pd.jaring.my

PT Hocatsu Pratama
Ruko Marina Mangga Dua Block C
7-8 Jalan Gunung Sahan Raya
No 2 Jakarta 10330
Tel: 006221 640 4777
e-mail: sales@hocatsu-pratama.com
Web: www.hocatsu-pratama.com

Central Plaza
1693 Phahonyothin Road
Lardprao, Chatuchak
Bangkok 10900
Tel: 662 937 1555
e-mail: property@centralgroup.com

Chatuchak Weekend Market
Off Phahonyothin Road,
across from Morchit Bus Terminal

united states

Asia Cook
Suite 30, 2850 Ocean Park Boulevard
Santa Monica, California 90405
Tel: 310 450 3270
Web: www.asia4sale.com

Bridge Kitchenware
214 East 52nd Street
New York, New York 10022
Tel: 212 688 42200
Web: www.bridgekitchenware.com

Broadway Panhandler
477 Broome Street
New York, New York 10013
Tel: 212 966 3434
Web: www.broadwaypanhandler.com

Dean and Deluca
560 Broadway
New York, New York 10012
Tel: 212 226 6800
Web: www.deandeluca.com

Global Table
109 Sullivan Street
New York, New York 10012
Tel: 212 431 5839

Gump's
135 Post Street
San Francisco, California 94108
Tel: 800 766 7628
Web: www.gumps.com

Joyce Chen Asian Cookware
20 University Boulevard
East Silver Spring, Maryland 20901
Tel: 201 593 8905

Katagiri
224 and 244 East 59th Street
New York, New York 10022
Tel: 212 755 3566

Pearl River Mart
277 Canal Street
New York, New York 10013
Tel: 800 878 2446
Web: www.pearlriver.com

Sunrise Mart
4 Stuyvesant Street, 2nd Floor
New York, New York 10003
Tel: 212 598 3040

Williams Sonoma
150 Post Street
San Francisco, California 94108
Tel: 415 362 6904
Web: www.williams-sonoma.com

Zabar's
2245 Broadway
New York, New York 10024
Tel: 212 496 1234
Web: www.zabars.com

useful websites

www.crateandbarrel.com
www.deliciousindia.com
www.ethnicgrocer.com
www.indiandelicacies.com
www.indianlife.com
www.namaste.com

bibliography

Andoh, Elizabeth, *At Home with Japanese Cooking* (Knopf, 1980)
Booth, Shirley, *Food of Japan* (Grub Street, 2000)
Davidson, Alan, *Seafood of South East Asia* (Federal Publications, 1976)
Dunlop, Fuchsia, *Sichuan Cookery* (Michael Joseph, 2001)
Gordon, Peter, *Cook at Home with Peter Gordon* (Hodder and Stoughton, 1999)
Hsiung, Deh-ta, *The Chinese Kitchen* (Kyle Cathie, 2001)
Kazuko, Emi, *Street Café Japan* (Conran Octopus, 1999)
Owen, Sri, *Indonesian Regional Food and Cookery* (Frances Lincoln, 1999)
Panjabi, Camellia, *50 Great Curries of India* (Kyle Cathie, 2000)
Simonds, Nina, *Asian Noodles* (Hearst Books, 1997)
Sreedharan, Das, *New Tastes of India* (Headline, 2001)
Todiwala, Cyrus, *Café Spice Namaste* (Ebury Press, 1998)
Tsai, Ming, *Blue Ginger* (Pavilion Books, 2000)

acknowledgements

AUTHOR: As a believer in karma, I would like to mention the propitious telephone call from literary agent Teresa Chris, who asked if I knew anyone who could write a book on Asian cooking tools. Without any false modesty, I said I could do it myself and so it came to pass that I met up with Jacqui Small to whom I give my most heartfelt thanks in offering me the commission.

Most of all I would like to thank my editor Jenni Muir for her inexhaustible patience, unstinting help in sourcing for guest chefs, and remarkable skill in making sense of my often convoluted copy. To art director Valerie Fong for her invaluable, brilliant artistic and cultural input, unflagging energy and logistical help throughout the hectic weeks of photography. They are simply the best professionals I have ever worked with and definitely on the A-list of my foodie guests.

I am also indebted to Tym and Tony Yeoh for their help in sourcing rare Indo-Chinese tools and their contribution of information on Thai culinary heritage. To all my family who turned their kitchens inside out for family-owned tools. To photographers Michael Paul and Nat Rea for their inspiring work in capturing the true essence of the food and tools.

Thanks also to my friends and fellow chefs, and the Blue Elephant Group in the UK for their guest contributions, to the chefs of the Raffles, Furama and Shangri-La Hotels in Singapore and all the chefs from the global front. Special thanks to Oriental City Supermarket, Colindale, Typhoon Europe Ltd, and Yoshikin (UK) for the loan of their items.

PUBLISHER: Thanks to Emi Kazuko and Roopa Gulati for help with photography, sourcing equipment and advice on culinary matters in their specialist fields. Betty Fong's help has been greatly appreciated.

We would like to thank the following for contributing recipes to this book *(in order of appearance)*: Fuchsia Dunlop, Peter Tsang, Deh-ta Hsiung, Ming Tsai, Shirley Booth, Emi Kazuko, Roy Yamaguchi, Peter Gordon, Elizabeth Andoh, Das Sreedharan, Cyrus Todiwala, Menernosh Mody, Yogesh Arora, Camellia Panjabi, Chef Chang, David Thompson, Marlena Spieler, Alan Davidson, Hong Sai Choi, Sri Owen and Neil Perry. All guest recipes are used with permission

index

(id) refers to ingredient identification pictures

A
All-purpose knives 13-14, 49
Almonds, Spiced lamb with 88
Aluminum steamers 29
Andoh, Elizabeth 67
Anise, Star (id) 80
Appam flour (id) 79
Aubergines (id) 78, 100
Aubergine salad with tart sesame dressing 67
Arora, Yogesh 97

B
Bamboo: leaf dumplings 107; leaves 103; mat
    for sushi 52; shoots (id) 12; skewers 122;
    steamers 28; wok cleaning brush 17
Banana leaf shaped plate 137
Banana leaves 102-103, 137
Banana leaves, Fish steamed in 105
Barbecued pork buns, 39
Basil, Thai (id) 100
Baskets: 69, 95, 118, 137
Baskets, Edible 124-127
Basket moulds 124
Beancurd, Fried (id) 48
Beansprouts, (id) 10
Bean thread noodles (id) 11
Beef rendang 120
Bench, Sushi 69
Bento boxes 69, 72
Bibimbap 70
Bibimbap bowl 69
Black beans, Salted fermented (id) 12
Bok choy, Baby (id) 10
Bok choy with oyster sauce 18
Bonito powder (id) 47
Booth, Shirley 58-59
Bottle, Soy sauce 41
Bowls 40-41; 68-69
Box, Bento 69, 72
Braising, wok 20
Braised five-spice belly pork 22
Bread making implements 89
Bread recipes: Barbecued pork buns 39;
    Naan 91; Paratha 90
Brochettes, North Vietnamese fish 116
Brush: Bamboo, wok cleaning 17; pastry 34
Buckets: Handled 23; Water 118
Buns, Barbecued pork 39
Burdock root 46
Burner, Tabletop 60

C
Cabbage salad, Vietnamese 114
Cake, cookie and snack tools 34; 113,
    132-136
Cake recipes: longevity 134; little sponge 136
Cashews (id) 79
Cashew nut and gomaiso dressing, Roast
    pumpkin with 66
Caramel walnuts, Peking-style 19
Cardamom, Green (id) 80
Carver, Japanese Kitchen 49
Carving tools 112
Chapatti flour (id) 79
Chapatti tools 89
Char siu buns 39
Chef Chang 106
Chicken recipes: black, double-boiled soup
    25; Claypot rice with salt fish and 27;
    Roast, Madurai masala 86; Yakitori 61
Chickpeas (id) 79
Chilli bean sauce, Fish in 21
Chillies (id) 47, 80, 100, 120
Chilli sambal, Hot 138
China 9-44
Chive flowers (id) 120
Chopping boards 13, 49
Chopsticks: 17, 40-41, 42, 68-69
Choy, Hong Sai 123
Cinnamon sticks (id) 80

Claypots 24
Claypot rice with salt fish and chicken 27
Cleavers 13, 14
Cloves (id) 80
Coconut (id) 78, 100
Coconut recipes: egg jam 139; Okra thoran
    83; rice 138;
Coconut-related tools: graters 81; wood
    tools 117
Congee, Prawn and spring onion 44
Cooling tub, Rice 52
Crimper and roller 132
Cumin seeds (id) 80
Curry leaves (id) 78
Curry recipes: green, with fish dumplings 108;
    Indian pastes 82; Nonya-style pork 131;
    puffs 133; Thai pastes 110
Curry pots 84-85
Curry puff mould 132
Cutlery 69, 137
Cutters, Cake, cookie, jelly and vegetable
    113, 132

D
Daikon: fresh white (id) 46, pickled (id) 48
Dashi 65
Davidson, Alan 116
Deep-fried ice cream 76
Deep-frying, wok 20
Dim sum utensils 37
Dishes, Sauce 40-41
Doc Cheng's 65
Double-boiled black chicken soup 25
Double-boilers 24, 128
Dough, Dumpling roller 34
Draining rack, wok 17
Drinks: Tea and sake sets 75
Drop-lid 56
Dumpling dough roller 34
Dumpling recipes: Bamboo leaf 107;
    fish, Green curry with 108, 111;
    Shanghai pork 36-37
Dumpling wrappers (id) 11
Dunlop, Fuchsia 21

E
Earthenware casserole 56
Edamame (id) 46
Edible baskets, Tools for 124-127
Egg noodles (id) 11
Egg recipes: Coconut jam 140; Wok-fried 138

F
Fans 52, 122
Fennel seeds (id) 80
Fenugreek seeds (id) 80
Fermented black beans (id) 12
Firepot, Korean 60, 63
Fish: balls (id) 121; cake (id) 121; knife/slicer
    49; scaler 112; shaped mould 113
Fish recipes: in chilli bean sauce, 21;
    dumplings, green curry with 108, 111;
    Kampuchean raw salad 109; North
    Vietnamese brochettes 116; salt, Claypot
    rice with chicken and 27; steamed in
    banana leaves 105; Steamed snapper
    with soy daikon fumet 65
Flower mould, Lompang 124
Fried rice, Yang Zhou 23
Fried tamarind-marinated mackerel 139
Fruit and vegetable carving set 112

G
Gai lan (id) 120
Galangal (id) 100, 120
Gas tabletop burner 60
Gochugang (id) 48
Gomaiso dressing, Roast pumpkin with
    cashew nut and 66
Gordon, Peter 66
Graters: 64, 81
Green curry paste 110
Green curry with fish dumplings 108
Green papaya salad 109

Green tea ice cream 76
Griddles 60, 84
Grilling equipment: Japanese and Korean 60;
    Indochinese 115
Grinding implements 64, 81, 108
Gulati, Roopa 88
Gyoza 37

H
Hibachi barbecue 60
Hibachi tuna with Maui onion salad 62
Hijiki seaweed (id) 47
Hopper press 92
Hoppers, String 93
Hot and sour prawn lo mein 43
Hsiung, Deh-ta 26
Hunan pots 24

I
Ice cream recipes: Deep-fried 76;
    Green tea 76; Kulfi 94
Idli pan 85
India, Pakistan and Sri Lanka 77-98
Indochina 100-118

J
Jackfruit (id) 78
Japan and Korea 45-76
Jelly: cutters 113; moulds 34

K
Kampuchean raw fish salad 109
Katori sets 96
Karahis 84
Kaya 140
Kazuko, Emi 61
Kimchee yangnyum (id) 48
Knives: Chinese 13-14; Japanese 49
Kombu seaweed (id) 47
Korea, Japan and 45-76
Kueh bolu 135-136
Kueh pietee 127
Kulfi moulds 92
Kulfi, Saffron and cardamom 94

L
Lacquerware 68-69, 137
Ladles 41, 95, 122
Laksa leaves (id) 120
Lamb with almonds, Spiced 88
Lassi, Fruit-flavoured 87
Leaves, fresh and dried 28, 31, 80, 100,
    102-103, 105, 107, 120
Lemongrass 100-103;
Lemongrass prawn satay 104
Lentils (id) 79
Lime leaves (id) 100
Limes, Kasturi (id) 120
Lompang mould 124
Longevity cakes 132, 134
Lotus leaf, Glutinous rice in 30-31
Lotus leaves 28
Love letter moulds 135
Lunch boxes 69, 96

M
Mackerel, Fried tamarind-marinated 139
Madurai masala, Roast chicken 86
Mandolin 64
Mangetout (id) 10
Mango (id) 78, 100
Mat, Bamboo sushi rolling 52
Materials, Choice of 7
Melon baller 132
Melon soup, Steamed winter 32
Melon, Winter 29, 32
Metal cups 29
Mirin (id) 48
Miso (id) 48
Mody, Menernosh 91
Mooncake moulds 132
Mortars and Pestles: 64, 81, 108
Moulds: cake 132; Chinese 34; Indian 92;
    Indochinese 113; street hawker 124;

Mushroom and leek spring rolls 35
Mushrooms: Chinese dried (id) 12; enoki (id)
  46; shimeji (id) 46; shiitake (id) 46
Muslim curry paste 110
Mustard greens (id) 10
Mutton, Tung Po 26

N
Naan bread 91
Nasi lemak 138-139
Nonya-style pork curry 131
Noodle (ids) 11, 47, 101
Noodle recipes: Chilled soba 73; Hot and
  sour prawn lo mein 43; fried vermicelli
  Xiamen-style 123
Noodle tools: slicer 23; soup bowl 40;
  strainers 122
Nori seaweed (id) 47
North Vietnamese fish brochettes 116

O
Okra (id) 78
Okra thoran 83
Omelette pan 56
Omelette, Rolled 58-59
Onion salad, Hibachi tuna with Maui 62
Owen, Sri 130

P
Painted baskets 137
Palak paneer 97
Palm sugar (id) 101
Pakistan, India and Sri Lanka 77-98
Pandan leaves 102-103, 120, 122
Paneer (id) 79
Panjabi, Camellia 94
Papaya salad, Green 109
Paratha 90
Pastry brush 34
Peanuts, Whitebait and 138
Peking-style caramel walnuts 19
Perry, Neil 131
Pestles and Mortars: 64, 81, 108
Pickle servers 96
Pickles, Japanese 50
Piette maker 124
Pineapple Fried Rice 106
Pineapple halves 102-103
Pistachios (id) 79
Plantain (id) 78
Plates: Dinner 40, 68; Banana leaf-shaped 137
Pork: Braised five-spice belly 22; curry,
  Nonya-style 131; dumplings, Shanghai 36-37
Pots: Chinese 24; Indian 85; Japanese 56;
  Southeast Asian 128
Pots, Yogurt 85
Potstickers 36-37
Prawn recipes: lo mein, Hot and sour 43;
  lemon grass satay 104; and spring onion
  congee 44; shao mai, steamed 38; in yam
  basket 126;
Press, Hopper 92
Presser, Chappati 89
Pressure cooker 128
Processing spices, herbs and coconut 81, 108
Puffs, Curry 133
Pumpkin and gomaiso dressing 66
Pumpkin shells 102-103

R
Racks: grill 115; wok draining 17
Radish, white, Daikon (id) 46
Red curry paste 110
Rendang, Beef 130
Rests, Chopstick 40-41, 68
Rice (ids) 11, 47, 80, 101, 121
Rice bowls 40, 68
Rice cookers 56
Rice noodles (id) 11, 101
Ricer, Stainless steel 92
Rice recipes: Bamboo leaf dumplings 107;
  Coconut 138; Glutinous in lotus leaf 30;
  Pineapple fried 106; Sushi 53-54; Yang
  Zhou fried 23

Rice scoops 52, 69,
Ridged griddle 60
Roast chicken Madurai masala 86
Roast pumpkin with cashew nut and gomaiso
  dressing 66
Rolled omelette 58-59
Rolling pins 34, 89

S
Saffron (id) 80
Saffron and cardamom kulfi 94
Sake sets 75
Salads: Aubergine with tart sesame dressing
  67; Green papaya 109; Kampuchean raw
  fish; Maui onion, Hibachi tuna with 62;
  Vietnamese cabbage 114
Salt fish and chicken claypot rice 27
Salt-grilled trout 72
Sambal, Hot chilli 138; (id) 121
Samosas, Lamb 98
Sandpots 24
Sashimi 51
Satay, Lemon grass prawn 104
Saucepans 128
Scaling tools 112
Scoops 33, 52, 69, 95, 96
Seaweed (id) 47
Serrated jelly cutter 113
Serving items: Chinese 40-41; Japanese and
  Korean 68-69; Indian and Pakistani 95-96;
  Southeast Asian 137
Sesame dressing, Aubergine salad with tart 67
Sesame seeds (id) 12, 47
Seviya mould 92
Shanghai pork dumplings 36-37
Shao mai, steamed prawn 38
Shiso leaves (id) 46
Shredding tools 81, 112,
Shrimp, Dried (id) 101
Shrimp paste (id) 101, 121
Sichuan peppercorns (id) 12
Sieves 95
Simmering pots 128
Simonds, Nina 43
Skewers 95, 102-103, 122
Small cooking tools: Chinese 33-34; Japanese
  64; Indian 95
Smoking, wok 20
Snack tools 33-34; 132-136
Soba basket 69
Soba noodles: chilled 73; (id) 47
Soy beans, fresh, Edamame (id) 46
Soup recipes: Chicken and mushroom 44;
  Clam and celery 74; Double-boiled black
  chicken 25; Miso shiru 74; Shrimp soup 74;
  Steamed winter melon soup 32
Soup: lacquered bowl 68; ladle 41; noodle
  bowls 40, 68; spoon 68; tureen 41;
Southeast Asia 119-140
Soy sauce bottle 41
Spatulas 17, 52, 64, 95
Spiced lamb with almonds 88
Spice storage 81
Spicy salads 109
Spieler, Marlena 114
Sponge cake moulds 135-136
Spoons, Porcelain 40-41
Spring onions (id) 10
Spring rolls, mushroom and leek 35
Square press, Flat 33
Sreedharan, Das 83
Sri Lanka 77-80, 93
Stacking basket 137
Star anise (id) 80
Steamboat 129
Steamed prawn shao mai 38
Steamers 28, 118
Steaming, wok 20
Stir-frying techniques 18
Stock: scoop 33; pots 24, 128
Storage 81, 118
Strainers 64, 122
Street hawker tools 122
Sugar, Palm (id) 101

Sukiyaki pans 60
Suribachi 64
Sushi 52-55
Sushi bench 69
Sweet simmered tofu 71

T
Tabletop burner, gas 60
Tabletop cooking 60
Tamarind-marinated mackerel, Fried 139
Tandoori skewer 95
Tart moulds 132
Tawa 84
Tea: cups 40, 75; ice cream, Green 76;
  Japanese 75; pots 40, 75; whisk 75
Techniques: banana leaves 105; cleaver 14;
  chopstick use 42; firepot 63; kueh bolu 136;
  longevity cakes 134; lotus leaves 31; paratha
  90; potstickers 36; rolled omelette 58;
  samosas 98; shao mai 38; stir-frying 18; sushi
  54; wok cooking 18, 20; yam baskets 125
Tempeh (id) 121
Tempura 57
Tempura pot 56
Teppanyaki griddle 60
Thailand and Indochina 100-118
Thalis 96
Thompson, David 108, 111
Thoran, Okra 83
Tiffin 96
Todiwala, Cyrus
Tofu: fresh (id) 48; fried (id) 48, 121;
  Scoops 23; Sweet simmered 71
Tongs 64, 95
Top hats 127
Trivet, Steaming 17
Trout, Salt-grilled 72
Tsai, Ming 35
Tub, Rice cooling 52
Tuna, Hibachi, with Maui onion salad 62
Tung-Po mutton, 26
Tureen, Soup 41
Turmeric powder 80
Turtle-shaped mould 113
Tweezers 113

U
Udon noodles (id) 47
Umeboshi plums (id) 48

V
Vadai maker 92
Vegetable: carving 112; cutters 113; knife 49
Vegetable stir-fries 15, 18
Vermicelli, fried Xiamen-style 123
Vietnamese: cabbage salad 114; fish
  brochettes, North 116

W
Walnuts, Peking-style caramel 19
Wakame seaweed (id) 47
Water bucket 118
Water chestnuts (id) 12
Whitebait and peanuts 138
Whitebait, Dried (id) 121
Winnowing basket 95
Winter melon 29
Winter melon soup, steamed 32
Wok-fried eggs 137
Wok: cooking techniques 20; sets 16-17
Wood tools 17, 52, 64, 95, 117, 122, 132
Wonton blade 34
Wrappers, Dumpling (id) 11, 101

X
Xiamen-style, fried vermicelli 123

Y
Yakitori, Chicken 61
Yamaguchi, Roy 62
Yam Basket 126
Yang Zhou fried rice 23
Yellow bean paste (id) 121
Yogurt pots 85